Life During
the Renaissance

Other titles in the *Living History* series include:

Life During the Renaissance

Hal Marcovitz

San Diego, CA

© 2016 ReferencePoint Press, Inc.
Printed in the United States

For more information, contact:
ReferencePoint Press, Inc.
PO Box 27779
San Diego, CA 92198
www.ReferencePointPress.com

LIBRARY OF CONGRESS CATALOGING-IN-PUBLICATION DATA

Marcovitz, Hal.
    Life during the Renaissance / by Hal Marcovitz.
        pages cm. -- (Living history series)
    Includes bibliographical references and index.
    ISBN 978-1-60152-802-5 (hardback) -- ISBN 1-60152-802-7 (hardback) 1. Renaissance--Italy--Juvenile literature. 2. Italy--Civilization--1268-1559--Juvenile literature. I. Title.
    DG445.M37   2016
    945'.05--dc23
                                                                                2015018996

Contents

Foreword

History is a complex and multifaceted discipline that embraces many different areas of human activity. Given the expansive possibilities for the study of history, it is significant that since the advent of formal writing in the Ancient Near East over six thousand years ago, the contents of most nonfiction historical literature have been overwhelmingly limited to politics, religion, warfare, and diplomacy.

Beginning in the 1960s, however, the focus of many historical works experienced a substantive change worldwide. This change resulted from the efforts and influence of an ever-increasing number of progressive contemporary historians who were entering the halls of academia. This new breed of academician, soon accompanied by many popular writers, argued for a major revision of the study of history, one in which the past would be presented from the ground up. What this meant was that the needs, wants, and thinking of ordinary people should and would become an integral part of the human record. As British historian Mary Fulbrook wrote in her 2005 book, *The People's State: East German Society from Hitler to Honecker,* students should be able to view "history with the people put back in." This approach to understanding the lives and times of people of the past has come to be known as social history. According to contemporary social historians, national and international affairs should be viewed not only from the perspective of those empowered to create policy but also through the eyes of those over whom power is exercised.

The American historian and best-selling author Louis "Studs" Terkel was one of the pioneers in the field of social history. He is best remembered for his oral histories, which were firsthand accounts of everyday life drawn from the recollections of interviewees who lived during pivotal events or periods in history. Terkel's first book, *Division Street America* (published in 1967), focuses on urban living in and around Chicago and is a compilation of seventy interviews of immigrants and native-born Americans. It was followed by several other oral histories including *Hard Times* (the 1930s depression), *Working* (people's feelings about their jobs), and his 1985 Pulitzer Prize–winning *The Good War* (about life in America before, during, and after World War II).

In keeping with contemporary efforts to present history by people and about people, ReferencePoint's *Living History* series offers students a journey through recorded history as recounted by those who lived it. While modern sources such as those found in *The Good War* and on radio and TV interviews are readily available, those dating to earlier periods in history are scarcer and often more obscure the further back in time one investigates. These important primary sources are there nonetheless waiting to be discovered in literary formats such as posters, letters, and diaries, and in artifacts such as vases, coins, and tombstones. And they are also found in places as varied as ancient Mesopotamia, Charles Dickens's England, and Nazi concentration camps. The *Living History* series uncovers these and other available sources as they relate the "living history" of real people to their student readers.

Important Events

1308
Dante Alighieri publishes *The Divine Comedy*, a poem whose definitions for good and evil remain pertinent in the modern world.

1352
Giovanni Boccaccio authors *The Decameron*, regarded as a masterpiece of Western literature.

1397
Giovanni di Bicci de' Medici moves his small family bank from Rome to Florence, laying the foundation for the Medicis to become the wealthiest and most powerful family in Italy.

1300

1400

1347
Bubonic plague arrives aboard a merchant ship docking in the Sicilian port of Messina.

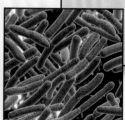

1477
Leonardo da Vinci completes his apprenticeship and opens his own studio in Florence.

1492
Roderic Llançol i de Borja ascends to the papacy, becoming Pope Alexander VI.

1378
Low-paid textile workers in Florence stage a revolt against the artisans and merchants for whom they work.

1494
Ludovico Sforza becomes duke of Milan.

of the Renaissance

1495
Da Vinci is appointed court artist by Ludovico and begins work on *The Last Supper*, which he completes in 1498.

1550
Florentine painter and writer Giorgio Vasari authors *Lives of the Artists*, which includes biographies of the artists of the Renaissance.

1665
Still a threat to public health throughout Europe, the plague kills seventy-five thousand people in London, England.

1503
Alexander dies and is replaced by Pope Julius II, who imprisons Cesare then banishes him to Spain.

1556
The city of Genoa outlaws slavery, leading to an eventual ban on slavery throughout Italy.

1500   1550   1600 ••• 1800

1517
Da Vinci completes the *Mona Lisa*.

1575
Three-year outbreak of plague in Venice leads to sixty-four thousand deaths—a third of the city's population.

1508
Michelangelo begins painting an interpretation of the book of Genesis on the ceiling of Sistine Chapel in Rome, completing the work four years later.

1861
The city-states, principalities, and kingdoms of Italy are united into a single country by Giuseppe Garibaldi.

1497
Cesare Borgia, illegitimate son of Alexander VI, allegedly kills his brother Giovanni and takes command of the pope's army.

Introduction

The Rebirth

The period of European history spanning from the early 1300s through the mid-1600s is known as the Renaissance, an era in which great advances in science, commerce, literature, and art were achieved. The Renaissance helped mark the end of the medieval period, which began in the fifth century when the Roman Empire, which had dominated life in Europe for more than five centuries, finally collapsed. During the medieval era new kingdoms formed, national borders were established, and the Roman Catholic Church exerted its dominance. But it was also a time when the expansion of Western culture, which had grown rapidly during the eras of the ancient Greeks and Romans, virtually stood still.

The Renaissance—a French word meaning *rebirth* and first used by historians in the nineteenth century—marked a new beginning for Western civilization.

Artists, writers, and scientists throughout Europe contributed to the Renaissance. In England, William Shakespeare established himself as the greatest playwright of all time. In Germany, Johannes Gutenberg invented the printing press, making books widely available to the masses. In Spain, the Greek-born artist El Greco established his adopted homeland as an important center for Renaissance art. The French mathematician and philosopher René Descartes perhaps best summed up the spirit of the era when he declared, "I think, therefore I am," suggesting that humans should use all their senses and powers of thought to define themselves and expand their knowledge.

WORDS IN CONTEXT

philosopher

A scholar and reflective thinker who endeavors to explain human beliefs and motivations and their consequences.

Born in Italy

Despite the contributions of the English, French, Germans, and others to the expansion of Western civilization, the Renaissance was born in Italy in the early 1300s. It was the Italian artists, writers, and scientists whose contributions helped humankind begin the path toward creation of the modern world. Among the contributors to the Italian Renaissance was the poet Dante Alighieri, whose 1308 masterpiece *The Divine Comedy* includes a dramatic tour of the underworld. More than just a fantastical journey through a mythological hell, the poem provides definitions of good and evil that still apply in the twenty-first century. "His vivid awareness of the deeps and heights within the soul comes home poignantly to us who have so recently rediscovered the problem of evil, the problem of power, and the ease with which our most God-like imaginings are 'betrayed by what is false within,'"[1] says Dorothy Sayers, a translator of *The Divine Comedy*.

The Italian artists of the era included Michelangelo, whose most famous work is his interpretation of the story of Genesis, painted between 1508 and 1512 on the ceiling of the Sistine Chapel at the Vatican in Rome; Leonardo da Vinci, whose masterpieces include the *Mona Lisa*; Raphael, whose most famous image is *Saint George and the Dragon*; and Sandro Botticelli, painter of *The Birth of Venus*. Says British art critic Andrew Graham-Dixon,

> It was in Italy, surrounded by the ruins of the ancient world, that men first dreamed of reviving the spirit of classical antiquity. Spurred by the melancholy conviction that their own era was a Dark Age, they sought enlightenment in the grandeur of once mighty Greece and Rome. They hunted out ancient texts and unearthed the tangible remains of the long-lost past. They brought the language of classical architecture back into use, emulated the sculpture of the antique world and attempted to revive what they imagined the lost traditions of classical painting to have been. "Renaissance," or *Rinascita* in Italian, was the word coined to express their thrilling fantasy of a rebirth, or a return to the first bright dawn of civilization.[2]

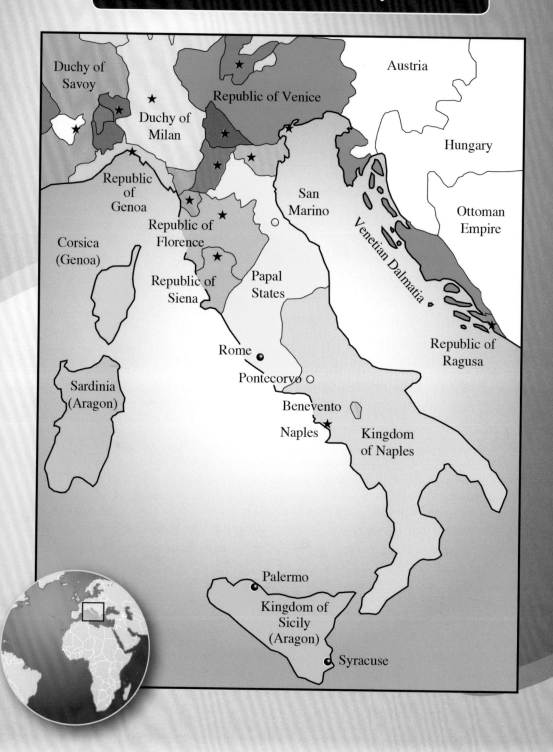

City-States of Renaissance Italy, ca. 1494

Duchy of Savoy

Republic of Venice

Austria

Duchy of Milan

Hungary

Republic of Genoa

San Marino

Ottoman Empire

Corsica (Genoa)

Republic of Florence

Venetian Dalmatia

Republic of Siena

Papal States

Republic of Ragusa

Sardinia (Aragon)

Rome

Pontecorvo

Benevento

Naples

Kingdom of Naples

Palermo

Kingdom of Sicily (Aragon)

Syracuse

12

Wealthy and Poor

Renaissance Italy was more than just a center of artistic and scholarly culture. During the era, Italy was populated by a wealthy elite as well as many poor people who were forced to endure relentless poverty. Italian society also included a growing middle class composed of merchants, artisans, and professionals such as doctors and lawyers, many of whom enjoyed modest prosperity. Moreover, it was a society that embraced democracy as many cities rejected the rule of kings and princes and established popularly elected community councils.

At the time of the Renaissance the Italian people shared a common language and other customs, but Italy was not a single, unified nation: The unification of Italy did not occur until 1861. Instead, the Italian peninsula consisted of a hodgepodge of kingdoms, duchies, and city-states, and most of the land was owned by the wealthy elite. Still, within Italy great and bustling cities grew—among them Florence, Venice, Siena, Genoa, Milan, Pisa, Naples, and Rome.

It was also a time of conflict. While wars among the cities or principalities of the Italian peninsula broke out from time to time, internal strife was a way of life. Rich people plotted against one another, jealous of their rivals. The people of the era also faced hardships that they were virtually powerless to overcome. During the Italian Renaissance people received spiritual guidance from the Catholic Church, but many church officials—and even some popes—were not above the taint of corruption. And throughout most of the Renaissance years people feared the disease known as the Black Death, a pestilence that wiped out millions of lives.

Moreover, women enjoyed virtually no rights and had access to little in the way of formal schooling. Most marriages were arranged, especially among women of wealthy families. Observed Cosimo de' Medici, a member of the elite Medici family:

> **WORDS IN CONTEXT**
> **duchies**
> Autonomous territories ruled by dukes and duchesses, members of the nobility who inherited their thrones through birthright.

Women's misfortune seems to be a great one, and men have a great advantage: since no matter how insignificant and pathetic a man may be, when he takes a wife, he always chooses one who pleases him, or not take her at all; whereas a woman, without knowing what or why, is subject to the wishes of others and must take what is given to her in order not to have worse.[3]

Achievements of the Human Race

And yet, despite jealousy, corruption, disease, and inequality, the achievements of the Renaissance spread from Italy to other countries, eventually spurring Europeans on the path toward exploring other lands. The Italian explorer Christopher Columbus first sailed for the New World in 1492 during the height of the Renaissance. Columbus's voyage provided a direct link between the birth of America and the belief voiced by Descartes: that no achievement was beyond the intelligence and talents of the human race.

Chapter One

Patricians and Nobles of the Italian Renaissance

Perhaps no family offers a better example of the wealth and power wielded by the upper class of the Italian Renaissance than the Medicis of Florence. Members of the Medici family could trace their roots to the early 1200s, but it was under Cosimo de' Medici, born in 1389, that the Medicis emerged among the richest and most politically powerful families in Europe.

The Medicis were a banking family. The family's fortunes grew after Giovanni di Bicci de' Medici moved his small family bank from Rome to Florence in 1397. The Medicis were savvy bankers and soon garnered great wealth and influence in Florence. Giovanni died in 1428; his son, Cosimo—then thirty-nine years old—took over the bank, soon expanding the family's interests into farming and trade. Medici-owned businesses exported silk and woolen goods to Russia, Spain, Scotland, and Syria. The Medicis also imported goods for sale in European cities, dealing in such commodities as almonds, spices, and sugar.

To maintain his power and fortune, Cosimo was willing to resort to strong-arm tactics. In 1441, when a political rival, Baldaccio d'Anghiari, was believed to be planning a conspiracy against Cosimo, the Medici patriarch had his enemy tossed out of a very high window. Just to make sure Baldaccio did not survive the fall, Cosimo's henchmen chopped off his head. Says historian Will Durant, "Cosimo used his power with shrewd moderation, tempered with occasional violence."[4]

Supported by the *Popolo*

Cosimo was a patrician—a wealthy citizen of the Renaissance era who gained his status and influence through shrewdness, political savvy, and, as the disposal of his rival illustrates, ruthlessness. Cosimo was, however, not a titled aristocrat—a prince or grand duke, for example. Unlike patricians, these aristocrats did not have to work for their wealth and power. They were born into the class of nobles that held power in Europe for generations and, throughout the Renaissance, continued to enjoy the fruits of the privileged class. And just as Cosimo dealt with his rival, the nobles of the Renaissance were not above using violent means to hold on to their authority. Indeed, the Renaissance may have been a time of great advancement in the letters, arts, and sciences, but it was also a time of warfare. Rich nobles and patricians plotted and schemed to enrich themselves and had no qualms about using military might to achieve their goals.

Cosimo made many enemies among the wealthy patricians of the era, but the Medicis were respected by the common people. During the Renaissance many of the Italian city-states were governed by *Signoria*: community councils elected by the citizens. Mostly these councils were composed of wealthy patricians and aristocrats, although many councils granted seats to merchants, professionals such as lawyers, and representatives of the skilled crafts. Poor people could expect no representation at all on the councils.

Even so, under the Medicis tax laws often favored the commoners—known as the *popolo minuto*, or common people—much to the anger of the wealthy. When Cosimo's father served on the council of Florence, he pushed through an income tax that favored the poor and middle class and penalized the rich. When Cosimo supported similar measures to tax the wealthy, he raised the ire of patricians and aristocrats yet endeared himself to the commoners. Said the Florentine diplomat, historian, and rival banker Giovanni Villani, "The Medici

> **WORDS IN CONTEXT**
>
> ***Signoria***
>
> Community councils that governed many of the city-states of Renaissance Italy; members were elected, but most members were wealthy patricians or nobles.

Under patriarch Cosimo, the Medicis became one of the wealthiest and most influential families in Europe. While notorious for his strong-arm tactics against political rivals, Cosimo was also a patron of the arts, using his fortune to fund everything from paintings to grand edifices.

were enabled to attain supremacy in the name of freedom, and with the support of the *popolo* and the populace."[5] Indeed, under Cosimo and his descendants, the Medicis became the virtual rulers of Florence, although the city-state was nominally administered by its *Signoria*.

The Titled Class

The Medicis did eventually enter the ranks of the titled class when in 1515 Cosimo's grandson, Giuliano, married Filiberta, the daughter of Phillip II, duke of the French region Savoy. Following the marriage the French king Francis I invested Giuliano with the title of duke of Nemours, a region in France.

Still, ascension of a patrician to the titled class was rare. For the most part the nobles of the era received their titles through birthright. The titled classes of the era included (in descending order) kings, princes, grand dukes, dukes, counts, marquises, and knights. The Holy Roman emperor—regarded as the supreme ruler over Italy and other European lands—actually reigned from Germany. By the era of the Italian Renaissance, when Italian city-states had raised their own armies and were homes to vast fortunes such as those possessed by the Medicis, it was not unusual for the *Signori* to ignore the dictates of the Holy Roman emperor and make their own laws.

Usually the titles of the Italian nobility were granted to the first-born males in the family. However, most families held a number of titles, so it was generally guaranteed that all sons would receive at least one title. If a daughter was born into a family that lacked male heirs, she inherited the title but passed it on to her male offspring. The wives of the title holders were known as queens, princesses, duchesses, countesses, and so on. They were respected as members of the titled classes; however, their husbands wielded the true authority in their families.

The Borgias

While the Medicis best reflected the wealth and power of the patrician class in Renaissance Italy, it was the Borgias, particularly the nobleman and general Cesare Borgia, who perhaps best symbolize the status of the era's titled class. For many members of the titled class, the Renaissance was a time of lust, jealousy, backstabbing, corruption, thievery, and murder. It is likely that no family pursued these sins with as much verve as

Looking Back

Florence: Cultural Capital of the Renaissance

Although many cities prospered during the Italian Renaissance, it was the city of Florence in northern Italy that drew the most wealth and therefore set the pace for the culture and achievements of the other Renaissance cities. Says historian Will Durant,

> [The Renaissance] made its first home in Florence. . . . Through the organization of its industry, the extension of her commerce, and the operation of her financiers, Fiorenza—the City of Flowers—was in the fourteenth century the richest town in the peninsula, excepting Venice. But while the Venetians in that age gave their energies almost entirely to the pursuit of pleasure and wealth, the Florentines, possibly through the stimulus of a turbulent semidemocracy, developed a keenness of mind and wit, and a skill in every art, that made their city by common consent the cultural capital of Italy. The quarrels of the factions raised the temperature of life and thought, and rival families contended in the patronage of art as well as in the pursuit of power.

Will Durant, *The Renaissance: The Story of Civilization, Part V.* New York: Simon & Schuster, 1953, p. 69.

the Borgias. "So many bizarre stories have been handed down about this hot-blooded . . . family that it is impossible, after five centuries, to know where the line of credibility should be drawn," says William Manchester, historian at Wesleyan College in Connecticut. "Much of what we have is simply what was accepted as fact at the time."[6]

The Borgias traced their roots to Spain. Cesare's grandfather, Jofré de Borja y Escrivà, was a nobleman from the Spanish city of Valencia. Cesare's father was Roderic Llançol i de Borja, who served as the archbishop of Valencia and, in 1492, ascended to the papacy as Pope Alexander VI.

Alexander is considered to have been a corrupt pope—it is said he won the papacy by bribing seventeen of the twenty-two cardinals who cast their votes in the papal election. After his election as pope, one of the Medicis, Lorenzo de' Medici, had this to say about Alexander: "Now we are in the power of a wolf, the most rapacious perhaps that this world has ever seen. And if we do not flee, he will inevitably devour us all."[7]

Indeed, during his eleven-year papacy Alexander is considered to have been primarily interested in enhancing his personal fortune. In describing the wealth of Alexander, the Vatican secretary Jacopo da Volterra, writes,

> His papal office, his numerous abbeys in Italy and Spain, and his three bishoprics in Valencia, Porto, and Cartagena, yield him a vast income, and it is said that the office of Vice-Chancellor alone brings him in 8000 gold florins. His plate, his pearls, his stuffs embroidered with silk and gold, and his books in every department of learning are very numerous and all are of a magnificence worthy of a king or pope. I need not mention the innumerable bed-hangings, the trappings for his horses . . . nor his magnificent wardrobe, nor the vast amount of gold coin in his possession.[8]

Alexander died at the age of seventy-three amid rumors that he was poisoned by his enemies. He is said to have left behind as many as eleven illegitimate children.

WORDS IN CONTEXT

florins

Gold coins minted in the city of Florence.

In Their Own Words

How to Do the Reverence

To learn the dances of the era, many ladies and gentleman of the Italian Renaissance turned to Fabritio Caroso, the most esteemed dance master of Rome. In 1600 Caroso authored a guide for student dancers, explaining the Reverence—a show of respect a gentleman was expected to display to a lady before beginning the dance. Not quite a bow, the Reverence instead required the gentleman to first remove his hat, kiss the lady's hand, then slightly bend his legs:

> You must, at the beginning of the music, slightly raise the toe of your left foot (which is forward), and then move it straight back in the time of two beats of music; then note, in moving your left foot back, its toes are even with your right heel; now keep [your foot] flat on the ground, and do not raise your heel at all. Do not do this on your toes, nor draw [your left foot] back too far, nor separate it, as some do habitually and who, by spreading their knees too far apart, appear to be preparing to urinate; nor must you cross the aforesaid foot behind your right, because all of this behavior looks extremely ugly to those around you.

Quoted in Julia Sutton, trans., *Courtly Dance of the Renaissance: A New Translation and Edition of the Nobiltà di Dame (1600) by Fabritio Caroso*. Mineola, NY: Dover, 1995, p. 98.

The Pope's General

One of his illegitimate sons was Cesare, born in 1475. Soon after Alexander attained the papacy he appointed his son a cardinal. Cesare displayed little interest in church politics or succeeding his father as pope. Moreover, Alexander favored Cesare's older brother Giovanni, appointing Giovanni to head the military forces of the papacy. (During the Renaissance and beyond, and for some three hundred years before the era, the pope presided over territory known as the Papal States, which comprised four Italian provinces. To maintain the pope's sovereignty the Papal States were defended by an army.) In 1496 Giovanni did not disappoint Alexander when he put down a rebellion of nobles against his father.

But a year later Giovanni was dead—the victim of a slaying. Stabbed nine times, his body was found floating in Rome's Tiber River. The crime was never solved, but a jealous Cesare has always been regarded as a prime suspect. Another motive is said to be Cesare's belief that Giovanni was carrying on an incestuous relationship with the brothers' beautiful sister, Lucrezia.

With Giovanni out of the way, Cesare elected to pursue his own military career. He resigned as cardinal and married Charlotte d'Albert. She was the sister of John III, the king of Navarre, a region in Spain. Now head of the pope's army, Cesare swept through Italy, conquering the armies of nobles whom Alexander regarded as enemies. Many of these principalities and minor kingdoms fell quickly, and when they did Cesare seized the titles and wealth that had been held by the defeated nobles. By the early 1500s he assumed the titles of prince of the Italian cities of Andria and Venafro; duke of the French region of Valentinois; duke of the Italian region of Romagna; count of the French region of Diois; and lord of the Italian towns of Piombino, Camerino, and Urbino. All had been led by nobles hostile to Alexander. When these territories were conquered, their armies joined the forces under the control of Cesare, making him one of the most powerful generals in the Renaissance world. In 1502 the diplomat and writer Niccolò Machiavelli said of Cesare,

> This lord is splendid and magnificent, and is so bold that there is no enterprise so great that it does not seem to him small. To gain glory and dominions he robs himself of repose, and knows neither danger nor fatigue. He comes to a place before his intentions are understood. He makes himself well liked among his soldiers, and has chosen the best men in Italy. These things make him victorious and formidable, with the aid of perpetual good fortune.[9]

The Fall of Cesare

A year after Machiavelli wrote those words, Cesare's power began to crumble. His father died in 1503, and the new pope, Julius II, proved himself no friend of the Borgias. Cesare fell gravely ill himself—he was believed to have suffered from malaria—and after recovering was forced to put down a revolt at the Italian city of Perugia. For Cesare, it turned out to be a rare military failure—perhaps because Cesare's judgment as a strategist was impaired by the lingering effects of the illness.

After suffering the defeat, Julius ordered Cesare to return to Rome, where he was placed under arrest. In 1504 Julius exiled Cesare to Spain, where he was imprisoned for two years but finally freed, probably at the urging of his wife's brother, the king of Navarre.

Cesare fought one final battle. Now in the service of John III, Cesare led an attack on a rebellious count in the Spanish city of Viana. His Spanish soldiers turned out to be cowards, abandoning their general in mid-battle. On March 12, 1507, at the age of thirty-one, he was cut down in battle. Says Durant, "It was an honorable end to a questionable life."[10]

WORDS IN CONTEXT

piano nobile

In the palace of a wealthy noble or patrician, the floor reserved for the occupancy of the owner—in most cases the third floor.

Displays of Wealth

Although nobles and patricians such as Cesare Borgia and Cosimo de' Medici spent much of their time enmeshed in intrigues and plots to enrich themselves, life for the era's wealthiest families could be filled with many pleasures. They traveled widely, kept mistresses, enjoyed the finest foods and wines, and lived in splendor, occupying opulent palaces, or *palazzi*.

The palaces of the patricians and nobles were largely located in the cities. In such a home it was not unusual for a wealthy resident to rent out lower floors to shopkeepers or artisans. Typically, the first floor featured the shops. The proprietors of the shops lived on the second floor, the mezzanine. On the third floor—the *piano nobile*, or noble floor—resided the wealthy patrician or noble. Living on the next floor above may have been lesser members of the household—sons or daughters or other relatives—and above them, on the highest floors, the household servants found their quarters.

Palaces were as ornate as their owners could afford. They might feature magnificent paintings or sculptures rendered by the Renaissance artists of the era. Each palace featured the *sala*—a large room set aside for dining and entertainment. The architecture was ornamental—the owners wanted outsiders to know that a wealthy and important citizen lived there. It was not unusual for the owners of urban palaces to buy adjoining homes and have them knocked down, then plant ornate gardens or erect public squares in their place as displays of wealth.

Palace of the Davanzatis

Typical of the era was the palace in Florence of the Davanzati family, patricians who made their fortunes as wool traders. The palace was built in the mid-fourteenth century by another family, the Davizzis, then purchased in 1578 by the Davanzatis. The façade of the home—the front outer wall—featured a loggia, or open area under a roof. As was the custom, the Davanzatis leased space beneath the loggia to shop owners.

Inside the front entrance—and closed off from the shop owners and their customers—visitors found an open courtyard leading into the home. At the far end of the courtyard, a wooden staircase took visitors to each of the palace's four floors. Each floor featured a *sala* as well as bedrooms and meeting rooms known as *madornales*. Also, each floor featured *agiamenti*—toilets, a rare luxury in the era. (These were, of course, not flush toilets, which had not yet been invented. But the architects of the palace designed a drainage system that funneled the waste outside the mansion walls.)

Another luxury of the era was the awnings that covered the windows, shielding occupants from hot sunlight. And the window openings were covered in glass—rare even in the most ornate palaces. In most cases cotton sheets covered window openings. (Occasionally, though, even the Davanzatis had to give in to practical needs and permit their servants to run clotheslines from the windows to dry the laundry.) Another luxury

Florence's Palace of the Davanzatis featured a splendid interior courtyard with grand vaulted ceilings. These elements were common in the fourteenth century when the Davizzi family constructed the home by joining together adjacent medieval structures.

found in the palace was a fireplace in nearly every room—installed to keep residents and visitors warm in winter months.

The floors featured stone tiles known as *cotto*. The ceilings were finished in polished wood. On the walls visitors found paintings or frescoes—images rendered directly onto the plaster. In the Davanzati palace the frescoes featured brightly colored scenes of trees, plants, and birds. Walls that were not decorated with frescoes were frequently adorned with woven tapestries. Even the furniture was decorated with art. Wooden chests known as *cassoni* could be found in every room. The chests were decorated with paintings; even the insides of the lids featured painted scenes. Statues or busts were placed throughout the rooms, as were birdcages. Headboards of beds were painted with images as well, and the beds themselves were canopied and as much as twelve feet wide: big enough for four people to sleep side by side. The bed sheets were linen—an expensive luxury in the era. The mattresses were stuffed with feathers. And pierced globes hanging from the ceilings were filled with burning herbs to provide the bedrooms with sweet aromas.

Turning Point in Fashion

The closets of the *palazzo* were likely to feature articles of clothing that were expensive and lavish. Indeed, the Italian Renaissance represented an important turning point in fashion. Throughout the medieval era clothes were simple and unadorned, even for the wealthy. But during the Renaissance patricians and nobles used their wealth to commission ornate garments for themselves.

Men wore brightly colored tunics with high collars. Gold chains hung about their necks. Pants were tight-knit hose. A loose-fitting, colorful, and ornately decorated outer gown may have been worn as well. Hats were decorated with feathers and jewels. Silk scarves may have been a part of a man's wardrobe.

During the medieval age women wore gowns that draped over their bodies, but during the Renaissance their gowns displayed the curves of their figures. The bodice, covering the body from the hips to the shoulders, was tight, but the gown was long and loose and trailed behind the woman in a train. Sleeves could be wide and loose or designed to be worn tightly over the arms. Women of Florence, in the north of Italy, tended to wear low-cut gowns. The women of Rome, in the south, wore gowns with higher necklines in deference to the modest taste in fashion preferred by the pope and other church officials. In fact, there is evidence to suggest the leaders of the Catholic Church did not agree with the direction in which women's fashion seemed to be heading in Italy. In the late 1200s or early 1300s a Catholic friar and historian, Salimbene da Adam, reported the concerns raised by Latinus, cardinal of Tuscancy, regarding women's clothing, According to Salimbene, Latinus suggested

Hieronymus Francken's sixteenth-century painting Carnival in Venice *displays the type of fashions popular among the city's nobility. Women's dresses had tight bodices and long, flowing gowns. Men wore silk stockings, ruffled collars, and decorative caps and hats.*

that if women did not adopt less ostentatious dress their sins would not be forgiven. Wrote Salimbene:

> Cardinal Latinus, the Pope's legate in Tuscany, put all women into a state of great distress by forbidding them to wear trains. Otherwise, they should have no absolution; and a woman told me that she preferred the train to all other garments she wore upon herself. Besides, the Cardinal gave order that all women, maidens, ladies, married women as well as widows and matrons, should wear veils over their faces, and that was horribly distasteful to them.[11]

Marzipan and Murder

Women wore their finest gowns for the many banquets and balls staged among the wealthy during the Renaissance years. The banquets reflected the wealth of the host and could feature as many as twenty courses. Generally, the first course consisted of cold appetizers—such as fruits, nuts, or candies. The main course followed—usually meat or fowl. The meals were prepared as ornately as possible. If the main course consisted of peacock, for example, the bird was served dressed in its own plumage, its colorful tail spread widely. A servant might light kindling inside the beak, serving the bird so that flames emerged from the bird's mouth as it was brought to the table. Other meats or fowl that were typically served were chicken, capon, pigeon, veal, and pork. Swans were a particularly favorite delicacy.

Following the main meal dessert was served—with the cakes or sweets carved into sculptures and set on the tables before the guests. Marzipan—a candy made of honey and almonds—may have been carved into a tiny statue and wrapped in gold (real gold) foil. Pies might be placed on the table, and when a guest sliced a pie open it was not unusual for a live bird to fly out. As the guests filled their bellies they were serenaded by singers or musicians hired to provide entertainment for the banquet.

As the banquets, wardrobes, and palaces of the patricians and nobles illustrate, life for the wealthy people of the Renaissance could be comfortable, luxurious, and satisfying. But outside the sheltered world of their palaces the patricians and nobles were always on guard, for unscrupulous and jealous rivals were willing to kill even their own brothers to enrich themselves.

Chapter Two

The Middle Class

One of English playwright William Shakespeare's most beloved comedies is *The Merchant of Venice*. Set in the Italian city during the 1500s, the play focuses on the troubles of an unlucky Venetian merchant named Antonio who finds himself facing many of the typical problems of a Renaissance-era businessman: He has borrowed money to make a deal, but the merchandise he purchased may have been lost at sea. With creditors closing in and his business on the verge of collapse, Antonio laments his situation to his friend Bassanio:

> Thou know'st that all my fortunes are at sea;
> Neither have I money nor commodity
> To raise a present sum . . .
> Go, presently inquire, and so will I,
> Where money is, and I no question make
> To have it of my trust or for my sake.[12]

The Merchant of Venice is less about commerce in Renaissance Italy than it is about other familiar themes in Shakespeare's comedies: love, mistaken identities, and a comeuppance for the villain. Still, there is no question that Shakespeare accurately portrayed life in Renaissance Italy, as the merchant class in Venice as well as other Italian cities was active, vibrant, and growing. Some historians argue that the merchants of Renaissance Italy set the tone for how business would be conducted for centuries to come. "It was everywhere hard to deny the positive consequences of material [growth]," says Harvard University business professor Sophus A. Reinert. "Even churches and palaces, after all, rested on solid economic foundations. . . . From its truly planetary material imagination to its entrepreneurial empowerment of individual initiative and trade, just as in politics and the arts, the Italian Renaissance was an eminently economic phenomenon."[13]

Geography of Venice

Most of the Italians who transacted business in the Renaissance era made up a growing middle class. Their personal wealth was not on the scale of the Medicis; however, they were far from poor. Other members of this class were professionals such as doctors and lawyers as well as shopkeepers and skilled artisans. All actively participated in the commerce of the Italian Renaissance.

One city that has long been dependent on commercial trade because of the consequences of its geography is Venice. Located in the marshy confluence of the Po and Piave Rivers of northeastern Italy, Venice was built on more than one hundred islands separated by canals. To outsiders these canals and the gondolas that navigate through them paint a romantic picture of the old city, but to Renaissance Venetians the canals represented a constant obstacle to life. Unable to feed its people through local agriculture, Venice had to import its food as well as the other basic necessities of life: lumber, metals, cloth, leather, and other goods. And so Venetians turned to a merchant class to meet the needs of their city. Says Will Durant, "The political history of Venice turned on her economic needs."[14]

Meanwhile, the merchant class established itself in other Italian Renaissance cities as well. The fifteenth-century poet Benedetto Dei describes the busy commerce of the city of Florence:

> Our beautiful Florence contains within the city in this present year two hundred seventy shops belonging to the wool merchant guild . . . eighty-three rich and splendid warehouses of the silk merchants' guild. . . . The number of banks amounts to thirty-three; the shops of the cabinet-makers, whose business is carving and inlaid work, to eighty-four . . . there are forty-four goldsmiths and jewelers shops.[15]

Located at the confluence of two major rivers and the Adriatic Sea, Venice was built on several islands separated by canals. It thrived as a port and trade hub, and by the thirteenth century, it became the wealthiest city in Europe.

Broken Banks

In Florence, Venice, and elsewhere in Renaissance Italy, hugely successful entrepreneurs—such as the members of the Medici family—thrived. But most merchants were more like Antonio: modest businessmen one bad deal away from bankruptcy. In fact, the English words *bank* and *bankruptcy* find their roots in Renaissance Italy. Merchants typically negotiated deals from a *banco*—a wooden bench. When the merchant could not pay his bills, his angry creditors literally broke apart his bench. The modern Italian word for *bank* is *banca*, and the Italian term for *bankruptcy* is *banca rotta*—literally, a broken bank.

Indeed, negotiations with bankers, suppliers, customers, and everyone involved in a deal were often hard-nosed. In *The Merchant of Venice* Antonio finds himself agreeing to part with a pound of his own flesh if he fails to repay a loan. In actuality, the terms of a deal did not pose such harsh consequences for failing to pay on time. Still, businessmen could be merciless with one another in their negotiations. The sixteenth-century Italian economist Bernardo Davanzati describes what it was like to do business in the Renaissance as a debtor and creditor squabbled over a debt. As the argument indicates, the creditor is demanding more money, or lire, because the number of florins the lire could buy has decreased due to the higher value of gold at the time. Explains Davanzati:

> The debtor who owes a florin worth 7 lire says: Here is your 7 lire. The creditor replies: You need to give me 10 because, today that is the value of the gold florin. . . . The debtor replies: If I give you a florin worth 7 lire, as the paperwork demands, it is not a minor achievement. If the Prince has reduced the value of the lire, this is a common storm that we share together, and we are all in the same boat. Your lament is with the Prince.[16]

Latin Schools

As the debtor suggests in his argument, the transaction was recorded on paper. Merchants kept detailed records of their businesses, which meant they needed to acquire the skills to read and write and understand arithmetic. In the centuries prior to the Renaissance education was limited to the sons—and to a lesser extent, the daughters—of the very wealthy only. But members of the merchant class knew they would need to be educated to conduct business, and so the institution of education emerged as an important aspect of life in the Italian Renaissance.

Educational opportunities differed markedly by class. Wealthy patricians and nobles could afford private tutors for their children. Members of the middle class, on the other hand, had two choices for the education of their children: Latin schools and Italian-language schools.

In Their Own Words

Authority of the Guilds

Merchants and artisans of Renaissance Italy granted their guilds a great deal of authority. The guilds set prices, settled disputes, and ensured that members charged fair prices and otherwise behaved themselves. The charter of the Wine Merchants Guild of Florence, which was established in the late 1200s, explains some of the duties of the guild:

> The consuls, treasurer, and notary of the guild are required to assemble together wherever they wish . . . to render justice to whoever demands it. . . . [They must] hear, take cognizance of, make decisions, and act on everything which pertains to their office, and accept every appeal which is brought before them by whosoever has a claim on any member of the guild. . . . They must record [these acts] in their protocols and render justice with good faith and without fraud on one day of each week. . . . With respect to these disputes, the consuls are required to proceed in the following manner in any dispute or quarrel brought against any member of the guild. . . .
>
> [If the dispute] involves a sum of three Florentine *lire di piccolo* or less, the dispute is to be decided summarily by the consuls, after the parties have sworn an oath, in favor of who ever appears to be more honest and of better reputation. . . . If the dispute involves 60 *soldi* or more, the consuls, after receiving a complaint, are required to demand that . . . the defendant appear to reply to the complaint. . . . Witnesses are to be called and interrogated in such major disputes, and the consuls must announce their judgment within one month.

Quoted in Kenneth R. Bartlett, *The Civilization of the Italian Renaissance: A Sourcebook*. Toronto, ON: University of Toronto Press, 2011, p. 59.

The Latin schools were aimed more toward the aspiring diplomats and writers of the era. The students read classic Roman literature, including the works of poets and philosophers such as Cicero, Virgil, and Ovid. As the name suggests, the lessons were taught in Latin—the language of ancient Rome and the language of the Catholic Church. Oration and rhetoric were skills taught in the Latin schools. Students read history—particularly the history of the Roman Empire under Julius Caesar. Graduates of the Latin schools were expected to go on to the universities of the era.

Only for Boys

While the students of the Latin schools were expected to pursue careers as writers, diplomats, and other professions of high status, the Italian-language schools taught classes of a more practical nature. Therefore, it was more likely that merchants, artisans, and professionals who wished to bring their children into their businesses would send their offspring to these schools. Students were taught to read—usually stories that taught them Christian values and morals. Mathematics, known as *abbaco*, was taught as well. In fact, some Florentine schools specialized in *abbaco*, for it was this skill that would do the student the most good if a father planned a future for his child in banking or commerce. *Abbaco* classes taught students weights and measures, currency exchange, how to calculate interest on loans, and how to set prices for goods. Teachers taught math in Renaissance Italy much as they teach math today: The emphasis was on problem solving because, as Antonio and any other merchant of the era knew all too well, business was full of knotty problems.

All of these classes were only available to boys because most were expected to follow their fathers into business. If girls received any education at all, it was at home. Wealthy girls were taught by private tutors; girls of more modest means were homeschooled by their mothers. And

> **WORDS IN CONTEXT**
>
> *abbaco*
>
> Mathematics taught in Renaissance-era schools in which emphasis was placed on calculating weights and measures, currency exchange, calculating interest on loans, and how to set prices for goods.

Looking Back

Life in Venice

Venice is unlike other cities in that it is built upon tiny islands connected by a series of canals. Although bridges and boats transported people from island to island during the Renaissance, most people tended to stay on their home islands. The two centers of activity on each island were the wellheads—the *vere da pozzi*—where people gathered every day to obtain fresh water, and the public squares, the *campi*. Says Garry Wills, an author and historian at Northwestern University in Chicago,

> The squares (*campi*) were the organizational centers of a city that originated as unconnected islets, each with its parish church or churches. At the beginning of the thirteenth century, the main node of Venice, the Rialtine land cluster, still comprised over sixty small islets, separated by more and wider watercourses than at present. Venice could not grow out from a central forum, like old cities of Roman foundation, or grow inward from containing walls. It was a multicellular accumulation of nuclei tied together by land ligaments or wood bridges or boat landings.

Garry Wills, *Venice, Lion City: The Religion of an Empire*. New York: Simon & Schuster, 2001, p. 18.

while their brothers were learning math and reading skills that would help them navigate through the worlds of business or law, girls were taught such skills as cooking, cleaning, and sewing.

Girls were taught to read, but only because they were expected to read prayer books in church. Otherwise, girls were raised with the expectation that they would be wives and mothers, although certainly the wives of shopkeepers were expected to help in the shop. Advised the sixteenth-century Roman lawyer Silvio Antoniano, "I do not approve of [young girls] learning languages, oratory and how to write poetry together with young male children . . . nor can I discern how this could be useful to the common good, or for the particular good of these young girls."[17]

Scales of Justice

Still, whatever reading and math skills boys may have learned in school were probably of modest value when it came time to engage in the rough-and-tumble world of business. Since merchants who imported their goods often bought them in foreign markets, the political climate in those countries could affect business. Buying goods from the Middle East or Far East meant the merchandise would not arrive in Italian ports for months. All manner of catastrophes could occur in the meantime: Warfare or bandits in far-flung countries could disrupt delivery, as could problems at sea such as bad weather or attacks by pirates. News moved slowly in the Renaissance world. The merchant might not hear of a catastrophe that delayed or disrupted his shipment for months.

Given all the pitfalls of doing business and the pressure of competition, the temptation to take advantage of one's customers was strong, but the notion of cheating in business was not often accepted by the merchants of the Renaissance era. The Catholic Church admonished its members, the merchant class included, to maintain high moral principles. (Many of these Catholic leaders, Pope Alexander VI for example, did not necessarily follow their own dictates. They nevertheless insisted that their flock do so.)

Moreover, a familiar symbol found throughout Renaissance cities was that of Justitia, the ancient Roman goddess of justice. Justitia is depicted holding scales, which served as a warning to merchants that they would be judged on the fairness of their weights and measures. In fact, the city governments paid close attention to the merchants doing business in their jurisdictions, enacting laws to ensure customers were treated fairly and that weights and measures were properly regulated. Merchants found to be cheating their customers could be kicked out of town or jailed. These laws applied not only to the merchants who were buying goods in foreign markets and selling to local shop owners and artisans, but to the shop owners and artisans as well. They were admonished by law and custom not to cheat customers.

Fair Prices

To ensure customers were not cheated, the city governments appointed various officials to keep close watch over commerce. In Venice the *magistrati* (magistrates) were appointed to monitor the markets. Venetian magistrates as well as officials in other cities were free to establish their own rules to ensure business was conducted fairly. During the 1300s the city government of Siena appointed a *guardia segreta* (secret guard) to tour the markets. Members of the *guardia* were essentially undercover officers, appointed to look for fraud. In the city of Bologna the *magistrato dei college* (magistrate of the colleges) set prices for goods, ensured that all weights were accurate, and appointed officials to circulate in the public markets to make sure prices were fair. If the *magistrato dei college* found merchants selling goods for what he believed to be exorbitant prices, he held the power to lower the prices on the merchants' goods.

Most cities also issued seals, known as *bolle* (literally, bubbles), or certificates that ensured the goods were authentic. In other words, to obtain the seal or certificate of authenticity, a merchant purporting to sell silk imported from China had to prove to authorities the fabric was really silk and that he had really imported it from China. The penalty for selling fraudulent products was severe—buyers who purchased the goods were entitled to their money back as well as a 25 percent penalty assessed on the merchant. During the 1400s the city of Piacenza elected three officials tasked with the duty of examining wool sold in the city to ensure its quality. A separate official was elected to inspect gold

> **WORDS IN CONTEXT**
> *magistrati*
> Magistrates or minor judicial officials who monitored markets, ensuring fair prices were charged and quality goods offered for sale.

sold by jewelers and goldsmiths to ensure the gold was of the quality and weight promised by the merchants.

Markets Bustling with Activity

Many merchants prospered during the Italian Renaissance, but so did their fellow members of the middle class: the artisans, along with the doctors, lawyers, and other professions of the era. The artisans—known as the *artigiani*—were members of powerful guilds that protected their interests and ensured they paid fair prices for the raw materials sold to them by the merchants. Guilds also saw to other needs of their members such as ensuring their funerals were well attended.

The marketplaces of Florence, Venice, and the other Renaissance cities were bustling—alive with activity and customers. Nearly all vendors specialized in specific goods. Bakers prepared bread and pastries. Brewers made ale. Butchers slaughtered animals and carved their meat. Leather shops sold shoes and also purses, saddles, harnesses, and bindings for books. Woodworkers fashioned barrels and furniture. Metalsmiths made dinnerware. Other artisans made soap, candles, baskets, glass objects, birdcages, musical instruments, ceramic goods, jewelry, paper, musical instruments, weapons, and playing cards. And, of course, many cities were home to vibrant textile trades with many skills to learn: cutting, sewing, and dyeing, among others.

Doctors and Lawyers

Joining the artisans and merchants in the middle class were members of the professions, among them doctors and lawyers. Although doctors and lawyers attended universities, they were not necessarily wealthy. Of the two professions, lawyers were held in higher regard, probably because the merchants and artisans of the era were often in need of their services to settle disputes.

As with others of the era, lawyers joined guilds that set prices and established licensing requirements and standards for the profession. Lesser workers in the legal professions, such as notaries, also belonged

Butchers were one of the many merchants who plied their wares in Renaissance markets. Master butchers were well paid and respected members of their communities, leaving the cutting and dressing of meat to their apprentices.

to the lawyers' guilds. During the Italian Renaissance, as is largely true today, a notary administered oaths, served as witness for the signing of documents, and affixed seals to documents to prove their authenticity.

Physicians garnered less respect than lawyers largely because medical science was not very far advanced during the Renaissance era. In fact, many people who practiced medicine in Renaissance Italy were uneducated and relied on folk remedies. Physicians did have to attend universities and, upon earning their degrees, were licensed to treat illnesses. Physicians could bring their wives and daughters into their practice. Although banned from the universities, the wives and daughters of doctors could learn as apprentices, then treat patients under the doctor's license.

Keeping Their Hands Clean

A different class of physician, a surgeon, did not have to attend a university. A surgeon could learn his trade through an apprenticeship and was called on to treat wounds and set fractured bones. Surgery was regarded as a lesser profession because it was messier. Doctors preferred to treat patients with illnesses simply because they did not want to get their hands dirty. Amputating limbs and repairing wounds involved the spilling of blood, which no good doctor wanted any part of. Doctors typically wore long coats when seeing patients, and they were hardly of a mind to get blood on their coats. Milanese doctor Leonardo Fioravanti rebelled against this attitude and did perform surgical procedures on patients. Writing in the 1570s, Fioravanti explains why other doctors refused to perform surgeries:

> The physicians . . . didn't want to dirty their hands by touching sores. Just to keep their hands from smelling bad they separated themselves off from the most important part of medicine, which is surgery. Of course, they reserved for themselves the authority to give permission to use surgery, but they didn't want to concede to the surgeon the right to practice internal medicine.[18]

Doctors' Guilds

In addition to surgeons were others who engaged in the healing arts with no formal education in medicine. Apothecaries made and sold medicines, but these were home-brewed herbal remedies with dubious healing qualities. Another member of the medical community was the barber, who practiced medicine by bleeding his patients. This technique, also known as bloodletting, was performed under the assumption that a disease could be bled out of the sufferer.

Barbers were also licensed to pull teeth and, of course, shave beards and give haircuts. Even Fioravanti recognized the value of barbers. Visiting Venice, he said, "In this glorious city of Venice there are most honored barbers, I say stupendous in their profession, who are very competent in medicating wounds and curing infirmities . . . and other devilry that the young are made to suffer."[19] Nevertheless, given the dubious quality of medicine, many ill people relied on folk healers, some of whom claimed to possess magical healing powers.

Doctors joined guilds as well, but their guilds also included the lesser-ranked members of their profession: the surgeons, apothecaries, and barbers. Grave diggers, known as *becchini*, were also granted membership into the physicians' guilds, evidently under the assumption that the patients would eventually end up in their hands, anyway.

Modest Homes of the Middle Class

Whether they practiced medicine or law, baked bread or made barrels, or sold wine or wool, most members of the middle class could count on a life of prosperity and a comfortable, if modest, home. Certainly the homes of the middle class were far from ornate, dwarfed by the *palazzi* of the patricians and nobles.

First and foremost, though, each home featured a bed, for the bed was the centerpiece of the home. It was in the bed that the next generation of the family was conceived. After the birth the new mother was expected to remain in bed for several days. It was here that she received friends, neighbors, and relatives to congratulate her on the birth and see the new baby. Therefore, members of the middle class spent lavishly on their beds and furnished their bedrooms in order to leave good impressions on visitors.

> **WORDS IN CONTEXT**
> *becchini*
> Grave diggers; despite the nature of their occupations, they were regarded as members of the medical community and permitted to join physicians' guilds.

Moreover, to guard against thieves the family's valuables were typically hidden in the bedroom, usually under the bed. A thief breaking into the home at night was unlikely to disturb the sleeping couple by slinking under the bed in search of the family's jewelry or gold. Even so, it is likely the father kept his sword under the bed—just in case.

Everyone shared the bed—not only husband and wife but children as well. Visitors invited to stay overnight were offered space in the bed, if available. Since the bed had to serve many sleepers, it was large, although

This sixteenth-century woodcut was part of a field manual for surgeons. Many Renaissance doctors avoided amputations and other surgeries because they were messy and often ended in the death of the patient. Instead, doctors preferred to deal with patients who needed simple remedies.

it lacked the painted headboards, canopies, and linens of the beds of the patricians and nobles. However, many people did hang curtains from the ceiling surrounding the bed. In the summer the curtains helped keep the bugs out, while in the winter the curtains helped keep the warmth within. The affluence of the homeowner was often judged on the quality of fabric used to fashion the curtains.

With so much attention given to the bedroom, the rest of the house was often sparse and simple. Tables and chairs were the most common types of furniture found in the other rooms. In most cases, though, a single table served many purposes—it was used for dining, of course, but also for card playing. If a visitor stayed the night and no room could be found in the bed, the visitor may have been offered the table for the night. The chairs were simple: They were often just stools; chairs with backs were rarely cushioned.

For the middle class of Renaissance Italy, life held promise. Merchants had the means to educate their sons with the intention of one day bringing the boys into their businesses. Homes were modest yet comfortable, although bedrooms could be crowded at times. The guilds kept everyone honest. Law was turning into a noble profession, although the practice of medicine was regarded with less respect. Even so, it was a prosperous time for the people of Renaissance Italy, who helped make their country into a center for European commerce.

Chapter Three

The Lower Class

The people of Renaissance Italy were charitable. They established hospitals for the poor as well as orphanages for homeless children and soup kitchens to feed the hungry. In 1500 the city of Florence was home to seventy-three organizations devoted to caring for the poor. One of those organizations was the Confraternita della Misericordia, or Brotherhood of Mercy. Its volunteers went home to home, caring for the sick. It was not unusual for wealthy people and even those of the middle class to bequeath at least part of their estates to charitable causes. In some cities the governments devoted tax dollars to services for the poor. The church was also involved in looking after the impoverished. In Rome, the Santa Maria Catholic Church fed two thousand beggars each Monday and Friday.

The existence of such an extensive charitable network suggests that there was an abundance of poor people during the Italian Renaissance. In fact, this was the case. A large number of the people of Renaissance Italy were either destitute or unskilled laborers, or they were members of the agricultural peasantry who could barely feed their families. Moreover, by the 1300s the institution of serfdom had died out in Italy, but slavery was permitted under law, and many patricians and nobles did own slaves. Men, women, and children captured in foreign wars were shipped home to Italy to work as slaves in the *palazzi* of the wealthy. This population added to the already large numbers of Renaissance Italy's lower classes.

No Help for the Lazy

The large number of charities devoted to the poor illustrates how charitable principles were ingrained in Renaissance society. The Catholic Church admonished its members to look after the poor. Charity was also a message delivered by the philosophers of the era, who believed it was the responsibility of humankind to look after those less fortunate. Matteo Palmieri, a fifteenth-century Florentine philosopher and historian, writes in his landmark work, *Della vita civile* (*On Civic Life*):

> Those who have some natural defect or illness or of age, and thus not able to provide for themselves, deserve public subsidy. In the former case their misery should provoke compassion; in the latter case, if they are small children, their preservation is [at stake] . . . for the [future] comfort and betterment of the common weal; if they are old, those who have passed the prosperous age of human life should be aided charitably.[20]

But as for the lazy, Palmieri felt no compassion. "All others, who, on account of the forces of nature, are perfectly able to take care of themselves, should not receive sustenance from the *patria* (homeland), if first they have not placed themselves in its service," writes Palmieri. "Whoever of these is shiftless and without virtue [and] seeks welfare, deserves to be driven from the city; [such a man] is useless."[21]

Selling Their Children

Although Italians of the Renaissance era embraced their responsibilities to look after the poor, by no means were Renaissance cities welfare states. Orphans were often found begging in the streets; if they eventually found homes in orphanages, they were housed there only until they were old enough to work. Usually, around the age of nine, boys were sent to local artisans to labor as assistants and girls to local homes to work as housekeepers.

It was not unusual for poor people—as well as members of the middle class who may have suddenly found themselves without funds due to bankruptcy—to sell their children into the service of others. Boys and girls as young as six could be sent off to the homes of strangers to work as

This painting by Pieter Brueghel shows a Renaissance card game ending in a brawl. Street fights such as this were considered minor offenses at the time, and those involved commonly received only a fine as their punishment.

servants. In return parents received a fee as well as the relief of not having to feed and clothe their children. In most cases the young servants received meals and housing but no wages.

Some of Italy's poorest people were mercenaries: professional soldiers who made up the bulk of the armies during the Renaissance. During times of conflict they were always able to find employment, but when the city-states or kingdoms were at peace soldiers found themselves unemployed. Many turned to begging or crime.

Crimes of the Renaissance

Unemployed mercenaries were not the only citizens of the Renaissance cities who turned to crime. To ease their poverty poor people turned to burglary, theft, robbery, assault, and other crimes against members of the middle class. Nobles and patricians knew to be wary of the poor and protected themselves with armed bodyguards. Says former University of Cincinnati historian John K. Brackett, "The undisciplined (wandering) poor lived a style of life that many thought would produce a criminal class, dangerous to society, if their problems were not addressed."[22]

The streets of Florence, Venice, and the other cities could be dangerous places as thugs lurked along darkened streets, ready to relieve a merchant of his day's earnings. Among the criminals found in the Renaissance era were petty thieves such as lowly apprentices and servants who stole from their employers. Another common criminal was the traveling thief who checked into an inn, then waited until the other guests had fallen asleep. The thief would then slink from room to room, rifling through the pockets of the sleeping guests. Sometimes these thieves stole more than coins. It was not unusual for a guest to wake in the morning to find his clothes had been stolen. Burglars breaking into houses stole food, tablecloths, knives, forks, and spoons.

> **WORDS IN CONTEXT**
>
> *podestà*
>
> An official who served as prosecutor, judge, and police chief, charged with enforcing criminal laws and passing sentences on wrongdoers.

Behind the house tools and even livestock were stolen from the shed or barn. Shopkeepers had to be wary of thieves who broke into their places of business to steal their wares, such as textiles and precious metals.

The *Podestà*

To deal with the criminal elements of its city, the *Signoria* appointed a *podestà*—an official who served as judge, prosecutor, and chief of police. (The term has its roots in the Latin word *potestas*, which means "power.") Typically, the podestà was a lawyer. To ensure the podestà acted fairly and was above corruption, the *Signoria* usually hired a podestà from another city. The podestà would then recruit local officers to work under him and enforce the law.

Although the podestà was considered above corruption, that assump-

In Their Own Words

Famine in Bologna

After several seasons of drought, as well as the spread of a fungus that further damaged crops, many cities in northern Italy were struck by a famine starting in 1590. Conditions were particularly severe in the city of Bologna, where many poor people faced starvation. The Bolognese patrician Pompeo Vizzani explains how authorities in the city took steps to ensure that poor people would not go hungry and that ill people received medical care:

> Every day in different parts of the surroundings of the city four ounces of rice [were] handed out to each of them, so that they could be protected from hunger until spring arrived, and then [officials had] the very poorest of the city listed for them by the curates of the parishes, and having prepared a list of up to ten thousand, took the decision to support them with great piety for eight months, that is until the next harvest . . . and similarly ordered that infinite numbers of the needy, who due to the hardships endured and to hunger, had fallen ill and were weak, be assembled and cared for with an increase in an infinite number of beds not only in the hospitals where they already previously were wont to look after the sick, but also in those appointed to house pilgrims.

Quoted in Christine Calvert, trans., *Guido Alfani's Calamities and the Economy in Renaissance Italy: The Grand Tour of the Horsemen of the Apocalypse.* New York: Palgrave Macmillan, 2013, p. 62.

tion did not often apply to the officers under his command. The pay for a police officer was low, and so the podestà was forced to recruit unemployed ruffians who were usually no more than common criminals themselves. They had little discipline, readily accepted bribes, and often committed crimes themselves. A typical ruse committed by a member of the police was to break into a house, claiming to be in search of law-breakers. Instead, the officer helped himself to the owner's possessions. Women of the house had much to fear from the police, as many women were raped during such incidents.

When they did catch a lawbreaker, the police had no qualms about meting out rough treatment during the arrest. Suspects were bound by the hands, beaten, and pushed through the streets to await trial.

Trial and Torture

Trial before the podestà could be a harrowing experience. The trial was held in secret, and the accused often did not know the charge that had been leveled against him or her. If the evidence was scant, the podestà sought a confession—often by torture. The most common form of torture imposed in a Renaissance court was the *strappado*—torture with a rope. Typically, the accused's hands were tied behind his back. The rope was then tossed over a ceiling beam and the suspect hoisted onto his toes. If the accused criminal refused to answer a question—or provided an answer that was unsatisfactory to the podestà—the podestà might order his officers to give the rope a yank.

Women were not subjected to the *strappado*, but the podestà employed many devices that could easily coax confessions out of reluctant female suspects. Various mechanical instruments were employed around the fingers that when squeezed could induce significant pain.

> **WORDS IN CONTEXT**
> *strappado*
> A method of torture in which a suspect's hands are bound behind his back, then hoisted aloft by a rope so that he is standing on his toes. With a yank of the rope, the suspect is lifted off the floor and, invariably, convinced to talk.

Other prisoners might be forced to stand for hours in uncomfortable positions. However the suspects were forced to bear their trials, virtually all eventually confessed.

Punishing the Criminals

Following their trials the convicted criminals faced their punishments. As Italy and the other European nations emerged from the Middle Ages, punishments were still quite severe. Capital punishment—usually through hanging—was imposed for any number of crimes from murder to minor theft. Other severe punishments included burial alive, castration, blinding, and amputation of the tongue, lips, or feet. By the end of the fourteenth century, though, criminals were being shown much more mercy. Some minor crimes, such as participating in a street brawl, were punished with no more than a fine—particularly if the accused pleaded poverty (as many did.)

Other crimes that were punishable by fines were public urination, throwing water (clean water was regarded as scarce and valuable), and minor cases of vandalism. These crimes were punishable by fines of no more than fifty lire. However, somebody caught carrying a ladder at night could be fined five hundred lire because people who carried ladders at night were regarded as burglars who intended to use them to climb into people's homes.

More serious crimes, such as major thefts and assaults, were punishable by prison terms. Write Thomas Vance Cohen and Elizabeth Starr Cohen, historians at York College in Ontario, Canada, "Jail, itself, for Italians of lower station, was a frequent experience. A villager could spend a few weeks in the castle tower while raising money to pay a fine; poor townsmen could be locked up as suspects or even as important witnesses."[23] Moreover, governments were loath to support prisoners. In many cases inmates were responsible for paying for their own food, which poor prisoners found difficult to afford. Many were able to rely on friends or relatives to bring them meals, but those who had no help from the outside or money to buy their food often went hungry.

In Florence a tower known as the Bargello served as the prison. The

Now a Florence art museum, the Bargello—with its lofty tower—served as a barracks and prison during the Renaissance. The building also housed the sheriff (the bargello), whose position gave the building its name.

name *Bargello* translates into English as "sheriff." Prisoners shared the cells, which featured hard wooden benches that ran along all four sides where the prisoners sat during the day and slept at night. If there were more prisoners than space on the benches, some prisoners slept on the floor. No other furniture was provided in the cells. The cells on the ground floor featured wells that provided water for the prisoners. On the upper floors, though, water had to be delivered to the cells in buckets. However, the cells on the upper floors featured windows, and therefore fresh air, while the ground-floor cells did not. The Bargello held as many as one hundred prisoners, mostly men, although a report prepared by a prison inspector in 1587 noted that seven women were incarcerated in the jail.

Ciompi Rebellion

With so many destitute people living in the Italian Renaissance cities, it is no wonder that many of them turned to crime. Many of these criminals, as well as the law-abiding members of the lower classes, held much contempt for the wealthy patricians and nobles and even the merchants and artisans of the middle class. "These rich citizens were either the leading merchants or the owners of feudal estates in the vicinity of the city, many of whom built fortified houses in the cities and used their armed retainers [private armies] to enforce their will," says University of Missouri historian Charles G. Nauert. "Although at first their political dominance was taken for granted, their armed retainers and their fortified urban palaces made them a source of disorder. The far more numerous non-noble citizens—the *popolo*—resented their arrogance and violence."[24] In fact, the *popolo minuto* referred to their oppressors as the *popolo grasso*: literally, "the plump ones."

Still, acts of rebellion against the *popolo grasso* were rare, but there is one notable exception: In 1378 a group of poor people known as the *ciompi* staged an uprising against the rich and powerful in what is known as the Ciompi Rebellion. The term *ciompi* finds its roots in the French word *compar*, which means "comrade." Frenchmen who visited Italian taverns were overheard by the Italian patrons saying, "*Compar, allois a boir*," which means, "Comrade, let's get a drink."[25] The Italian patrons mispronounced *compar*, using the word *ciompi*, referring to one another as comrades.

> **WORDS IN CONTEXT**
>
> ***popolo grasso***
> Literally, "the plump ones"—a term of derision uttered by poor people when referring to nobles and patricians.

The ciompi were unskilled laborers who worked in the textile trades. Their pay was low, and many lived on the verge of poverty. Their bosses, textile makers of Florence, belonged to guilds that set prices for wool and other textiles, ensuring themselves handsome profits.

In June 1378 leaders of the ciompi presented petitions to the *Signoria*, demanding higher wages. The petitions were ignored. On July 22 the ciompi rioted in the streets of Florence. The ciompi easily overwhelmed

Looking Back

The Barnabites

One of the charitable organizations that worked among the poor of Milan during the Italian Renaissance was known as the Barnabites. This religious order was composed mostly of nobles who rejected their symbols of social distinction: their wealth, ornate clothing, and long beards. The Barnabites were established in 1535; the group drew its name from the St. Barnabas Catholic Church in Milan. Although the Barnabites worked among the poor, they were motivated more out of a desire to seek personal redemption before God than out of sympathy for the impoverished. Says Querciolo Mazzonis, a historian at the University of Teramo in Italy,

> Renunciation of status was . . . the main value behind the Barnabites' acts of public penance, such as wandering about poorly dressed and preaching in the squares of Milan with a rope around their necks or bearing a cross. Their service among the sick and the poor in the hospitals was part of their penitential exercise. . . . Thus, works of charity in hospitals or among the sick and the poor were not carried out merely to alleviate the sufferings of needy people but functioned as acts of penance, forms of public humiliation that enabled individuals to give up social honor and secular aspirations and thus become closer to God.

Querciolo Mazzonis, *Spirituality, Gender, and the Self in Renaissance Italy: Angela Merici and the Company of St. Ursula (1474–1540)*. Washington, DC: Catholic University of America Press, 2007, p. 149.

a small armed force, dispatched by the *Signoria* to quell the riot, and soon took control of the government. Niccolò Machiavelli describes the Ciompi Rebellion:

> The first body of plebeians that made its appearance was that which had assembled at [the church] San Pietro Maggiore; but the armed force did not venture to attack them. . . . Many citizens, to avenge themselves of private injuries, conducted [the mob] to houses of their enemies. . . .
>
> The tumult continued all day, and at night the rioters halted . . . behind the church of St. Barnabas. Their number exceeded six thousand . . . and when morning came, they proceeded to the palace of the provost, who refusing to surrender [the government] to them, they took possession of it by force.[26]

The ciompi installed one of its leaders, Michele di Lando, as the chief executive of the council, the *gonfaloniere* of justice. Di Lando and other ciompi leaders remained in power for four years, but they were unable to accomplish change. Their rule was opposed by the guild members for whom they worked, who did not want to raise their wages. They were also opposed by the wealthy patricians and nobles of Florence who also did not want to lose their profits to lower-class workers. The ciompi movement finally collapsed in 1382 after a series of street brawls in which the guild members outfought the ciompi.

The Peasant Class

As the failed Ciompi Rebellion illustrates, members of the lower classes of the Renaissance cities seemed to have little hope of rising above the poverty that ensnared their lives. In the countryside the poor peasants who worked for meager earnings were also trapped in relentless poverty.

Although Renaissance Italy saw the growth of large and bustling cities, as much as 75 percent of the population lived on farms, and the vast majority of the rural people were peasants. The peasant class of the Renaissance was a holdover from the medieval era, when serfs were bound to the land of their masters. Serfs, little more than slaves, were required to live on the land and raise crops for their aristocrat masters. As payment, the serfs were permitted to keep a small share of what they grew. Moreover, serfdom was inherited—a serf's descendants were bound to the land as well.

In Italy, as in most of Europe, serfdom died out in the 1100s and 1200s as the society turned toward a cash-based economy. Instead of crops, landlords preferred cash payments. And so they freed their serfs and permitted them to remain on the land and grow crops. In return, members of the new peasant class were required to pay rents to the landowners.

The system worked out much better for the landowners than the peasants. In addition to the rents, peasants were also responsible for tithes to the church (donations of a portion of their incomes) as well as taxes to the state. If drought or other unfavorable weather conditions struck the region and affected that year's crop, it caused a hardship. The peasants still had to pay rent and taxes and make their contributions to the church. In many cases peasants borrowed money to see themselves through difficult times. And if they failed to pay their debts, the peasants could expect to be sentenced to a debtors' prison.

Primitive Tools and Homes

To coax their crops out of the land, the primary tool owned by the peasant was the spade, for it was the peasant's job to break ground to plant grain. Under the best of circumstances it was backbreaking work, made even more difficult given the fact that the spades were made of wood. Tools made of metal cost too much for the typical peasant of the era to afford. In addition to grain, many peasants grew apples, apricots, flax, and beans. They also raised chickens and donkeys.

The typical peasant home was far removed from the city palaces of the *popolo grasso* or even the more modest urban homes of the middle class. The typical peasant lived in a one-room, sparsely furnished hovel. The home included a bed in which everyone—father, mother, and children—slept. Other furnishings included a crude table and chairs and perhaps a chest for storage. All meals were cooked in an iron pot hung in the fireplace. The home was likely to share a common wall with a barn or stable. The children of peasants did not go to school. Instead, as soon as they were able to

A scene from a peasant home shows many activities that defined the life of the poorer classes. Here, in a single room, family members cook, churn butter, nurse infants, and even receive gifts from visiting wealthy donors.

perform physical labor, their fathers put them to work in the fields. As farm laborers, boys were much more valued than girls because they were able to perform more work. Says Duccio Balestracci, a historian at the University of Siena in Italy, "Families living on the land considered the birth of a girl as a loss of two strong arms for the heavy work required by country life: at the very most peasant girls could carry out the lighter tasks in the household economy, such as pasturing the flocks or tending the courtyard animals."[27]

Born to Obey

Despite the hardships faced by the peasants, it was the slaves who were forced to suffer through the bitterest of existences during the Renaissance. Captured on foreign battlefields in the Middle East, they were sold to wealthy patricians and nobles mostly as household laborers. By the end of the 1500s it was estimated that some three thousand slaves were owned by patrician masters or nobles in Florence. This era also marked the beginning of the African slave market as the first European slave traders invaded Ethiopia and North Africa, captured slaves, and sold them throughout Europe.

African slaves were not put to work in the fields—as they would be in America a century later—but instead were used mostly as household servants. In 1488 one of the Medicis, Ippolito de' Medici, purchased one hundred Africans and had them trained as wrestlers. He then gave them as gifts to Pope Innocent VIII, who in turn gave them to cardinals, Italian nobles, and others who had won his favor. These slaves were used as entertainers, forced to engage in wrestling matches at parties for the bemusement of the wealthy attendees.

Whether the slaves were made to do physical labor or perform as entertainers for the patricians and nobles, the notion that slavery was wrong did not resonate with the Italians of the Renaissance era. The philosophy that slavery was an acceptable source of labor is summed up by fifteenth-century Italian diplomat and soldier Baldassare Castiglione, who says:

> Some . . . are born and devised and ordained by Nature to obey, just as others are to command. . . . There are also many men concerned solely with physical activities, and these differ from men versed in the things of the mind as much as the soul differs from the body. . . . These, then, are essentially slaves, and it is better for them to obey than command.[28]

Relentless Poverty

In Italy slavery started dying out in 1556 when the city of Genoa banned the ownership of humans, but this did not improve the lot of other members of the lower classes. Mired in relentless poverty, they were for the most part prevented from enjoying the fruits of one of the most dynamic eras of European history.

Chapter Four

The Black Death

A deadly contagion arrived in October 1347 aboard a merchant vessel returning from China, docking in the Sicilian port city of Messina. As the ship drifted into the harbor most of the crew was already dead. Horrified local officials ordered the ship to leave, but it was too late. The pestilence onboard had already spread into the city.

By the end of the fourteenth century the bubonic plague spread well beyond the borders of Italy, infecting people in virtually every country in Europe. By then some 3 million Italians—nearly 30 percent of the population of Italy—had died from the disease known as the Black Death. In all, some 25 million Europeans—60 percent of the population of the Continent—were victims of the plague.

And the horror did not end after the first outbreak. The plague resurfaced in Europe from time to time, killing millions more over the course of the next 350 years. In addition to the death toll in Europe, the plague also wiped out huge populations in the Middle East and Far East. In all, it is believed the plague caused 137 million deaths worldwide.

Virtually every family in Europe was touched by the plague. Agnolo di Tura kept a journal of the plague years in the Italian city of Siena. In 1348 he wrote,

> The mortality in Siena began in May. It was a horrible thing, and I do not know where to begin to tell of the cruelty. . . . Members of a household brought their dead to a ditch as best they could, without a priest, without any divine services. Nor did the death bell sound. . . . And as soon as those ditches were filled, more were dug. I Agnolo di Tura, buried my five children with my own hands. . . . And no bells tolled, and nobody wept no matter what his loss because almost everyone expected death. . . . And people said and believed, "This is the end of the world."[29]

Wrath of God

Bubonic plague is a bacterial disease spread by fleas hidden on the bodies of rats. As such, the disease is not spread from human to human through a cough or sneeze but rather by fleas that jump off the bodies of the rats onto human bodies and then onto other human bodies. Fleas leave the rats because the rats themselves are made ill and die from the bites of the fleas. Lacking nourishing blood from the bodies of the rats, the fleas seek their meals elsewhere, finding it on the bodies of human victims. Infected fleas spread the deadly bacteria *Yersinia pestis* by sucking the blood of their hosts, then infecting the wounds by regurgitating the bacteria.

But the cause of the plague remained a mystery to the people of the Renaissance, an era in which medical science was virtually unknown. As a result, fleas were not blamed for the plague. In fact, in France doctors at the University of Paris—regarded as the leading medical school of the Renaissance era—theorized the plague was caused by the position of the planets precisely at 1:00 p.m. on March 20, 1345. Proclaimed doctors at the university: "For Jupiter, being wet and hot, draws up evil vapors from the earth, and Mars, because it is immoderately hot and dry, then ignites the vapors, and as a result there were lightnings, sparks, noxious vapors, and fires throughout the air."[30] Others suggested the plague was caused by birds, frogs, rotten fruit falling from trees, large spiders, mad dogs, and mysterious vapors that rose from the soil. Many people believed it was the work of an angry God. "There is no health in my flesh, because of the wrath; there is no peace for my bones, because of my sins"[31] was an oft-quoted passage from Psalm 38 during the plague years.

Many victims sought redemption, confessing their sins in the hope God would lift the plague from their bodies. Wealthy Italians donated large sums to the Catholic Church to build new altars or entire cathedrals in the hope these offerings would spare them from the plague. It did not work. The plague struck all classes of people, rich and poor.

> **WORDS IN CONTEXT**
>
> *Yersinia pestis*
> The germ that causes the bubonic plague; it enters the bloodstream of victims through the bites of fleas that carry the bacteria.

Because they lacked sanitation and pest control, European cities of the Renaissance were rife with squalor and disease. Bacteria spread to human city dwellers through the bites of fleas that came in on the backs of rats.

Rats Roamed Free

Such a horrific disease spread easily in a culture where rats roamed free in the streets or hid in the nooks and crannies of homes, picking through garbage and other human waste. Modern plumbing was unknown in the Renaissance era—flush toilets did not go into widespread use until the late 1800s. People of means used chamber pots in their homes, which servants emptied into the rivers or streets. Others used community latrines, which were no more than large ditches.

Garbage was not collected—it was tossed into the streets, where it piled up and provided breeding places for rats. Inside homes, conditions were hardly sanitary. Only wealthy people could afford carpets made out of fabrics. In the homes of the middle class and the poor, if floors were covered at all people used mats woven from rush—a plant found in the marshes. Insects, including fleas, were known to infest the mats. Moreover, after a meal it was common for people to toss their leftovers onto the floor mats for the dogs and cats to eat. A lot of the garbage stayed in the mats, where it attracted rats and other vermin.

The rancid state of homes as well as city streets and other public areas was more pronounced in the summer months—a time when garbage and human and animal waste baked in the sun, drawing more rats. That helps explain why the plague seemed to strike more victims during hotter weather. "It was during the hottest months of the year that [people] smelled the foulest odors from the dirty streets, the faulty sewers, the sinks, the dung in the stables,"[32] says University of California at Berkeley historian Carlo M. Cipolla.

Plague Symptoms

With so much garbage and dung piling up and with rats seemingly everywhere, the plague spread quickly. Symptoms manifested themselves within a week of exposure to the bacteria. Chills, headache, fever, and weakness were common symptoms. Swelling throughout the body was common, mostly in the lymph nodes, which are found in the neck, groin, and armpits. These swellings are known as buboes—hence, the name bubonic plague. Additional symptoms included inflammation of the throat and lungs. The body emitted an unpleasant stench. In the final stages, just before they died, victims vomited blood. Most victims died within a few days of discovering their symptoms. In his 1352 book *The Decameron*, the Florentine writer and poet Giovanni Boccaccio describes how the disease affected its victims:

> **WORDS IN CONTEXT**
> **chamber pot**
> A ceramic bowl used as a toilet; typically it was emptied in the streets or rivers, helping to spread contamination.

> If any bled at the nose, it was a manifest sign of inevitable death;
> nay, but in men and women alike there appeared, at the beginning
> of the malady, certain swellings, either on the groin or under the
> armpits, whereof some waxed of the bigness of a common apple,

others like unto an egg, some more and some less, and these the vulgar named plague-boils. From these two parts the aforesaid death-bearing plague-boils proceeded, in brief space, to appear and come indifferently in every part of the body; wherefrom, after awhile, the fashion of the contagion began to change into black or livid blotches, which showed themselves in many [first] on the arms and about the thighs and [then to] every other part of the person, in some large and sparse and in others small and thick-sown; and like as the plague-boils had been first (and yet were) a very certain token of coming death, even so were these for every one to whom they came.[33]

Victims of the Plague

Effects of the plague went beyond the mere loss of life. Families collapsed as people fled their homes. Whole communities ceased to exist as towns and villages were abandoned. In cities entire neighborhoods seemed abandoned. In Venice fifty-one thousand people died just in 1575 and 1576. "Venice offered almost ideal conditions for its spread—it was a warm seaport with high humidity, just the kind of place where the black rat flea flourishes,"[34] says Garry Wills.

The plague played no favorites among rich and poor, talented and unskilled. Renaissance painter Tiziano Vecellio, known as Titian, died of the 1576 plague. Titian was not the only victim of note. Two other Renaissance painters who fell victim to the plague were the brothers Ambrogio and Pietro Lorenzetti. Other famous figures from the era who succumbed to the Black Death were Giovanni Villani and Giovanni d'Andrea, a noted expert on cannon law—the laws of the Catholic Church. Perhaps the most noted victim of the plague was the king of Sicily, known as Louis the Child because he ascended to the throne at the age of four. (The young king ruled under the authority of an adult regent until he reached the age of sixteen.) Louis died in October 1355, five months before his eighteenth birthday.

Whether the plague struck the palace of a king or the most humble of peasant dwellings, victims experienced terrible pain and anguish. Family members could do little but watch their loved ones die. Observing the plague sweeping through the Italian city of Bologna in 1630, the Catholic cardinal Bernardino Spada said,

> Here you see people lament, others cry, others strip themselves to the skin, others die, others become black and deformed, others lose their minds. Here you are overwhelmed by intolerable smells. Here you cannot walk but among corpses. Here you feel naught but the constant horror of death. This is the faithful replica of hell since there is no order and only horror prevails.[35]

Treating the Victims

Given the widespread suffering and mortality caused by the plague, it was clear that doctors of the era could do little to help the victims. Physicians suspected the plague was spread by close personal contact with the patient—and indeed, the fleas did leap from person to person. And so the prevailing strategy of the plague era called for locking the doors of a plague-stricken house, isolating the victim—and his or her family—from the rest of the community. Invariably this resulted in a death sentence pronounced upon healthy family members, for locked up with their suffering relatives they too were likely to contract the plague.

But even if doctors did make the effort to treat plague victims, there was little they could do for them because they lacked the modern drugs that are effective in curing plague victims. (Not until the twentieth century were antibiotic drugs developed that are capable of curing bubonic plague and similar infectious diseases.) At first, the preferred method for treating the plague was to remove the buboes. And so surgeons attacked the buboes with their scalpels, slicing them off the patients' bodies. This treatment proved ineffective and, if anything, enhanced the suffering of

A physician lances the buboes on the neck of a city woman. The bubonic plague, known as the Black Death, first swept through crowded European cities in the fourteenth century, killing roughly 25 million people. Smaller outbreaks flared up throughout the Renaissance.

the victim. Another popular method of treatment was bloodletting. Barbers were often called in to drain the plague victim of his or her blood, hoping the disease would leave the body along with the blood of the sufferer. Some doctors published manuals for barbers, showing them which veins to open—depending on the locations of the patients' buboes.

Bleed Just the Ruddy

However, by the mid-1500s physicians began to doubt the effectiveness of bloodletting. The French doctor Ambrose Paré traveled throughout his country questioning doctors, surgeons, and barbers. He concluded that some plague victims managed to recover—but not if they were bled. All plague victims who were bled died under their doctors' care, he found.

Other doctors drew similar conclusions and counseled their colleagues to draw less blood. Giovanni da Vigo, the personal physician to Pope Julius II, urged doctors to draw blood only on the first day that symptoms were apparent. On the second day, he theorized, the plague had infected a greater quantity of blood and, therefore, more blood would have to be drawn to treat the victim. Da Vigo suggested that drawing too much blood from the victim might further weaken the patient. This was somewhat of a radical notion, given that his viewpoint would not be accepted as a sound medical principle for many years.

Another physician of the era, Giovanni Battista Napolitano, recommended bleeding only large, strong, and ruddy men. The doctor was under the impression that men with ruddy complexions were blessed with blood to spare, and therefore bleeding the plague out of them could be a viable treatment. He was, of course, wrong.

By the 1570s most doctors had concluded that bleeding was not the answer, and so they turned to the apothecaries for cures. But since medicines were home-brewed concoctions of herbs and other natural substances, these remedies did not work. Plague victims were given doses of poison in the hope that the disease would be neutralized. Many times the poisons just hastened the deaths of the patients. Another treatment involved giving the patient an herbal laxative in the hope the disease would be purged from the body in that fashion. Some apothecaries prepared salves and ointments to be applied directly to the buboes. These were ineffective as well.

Preventing the Plague

Although doctors were at a loss to find effective treatments for the plague, some hoped to prevent the spread of the disease. For the most part, however, their methods fell short of success. Some doctors promoted the use

In Their Own Words

Devoured by Fleas

In 1657 Father Antero Maria da San Bonaventura, a Catholic priest who administered a hospital for plague victims in Genoa, directed all hospital workers to wear long robes covered in wax, believing wax repelled the disease. The wax was also treated with spices in the belief the scents purified the air inhaled by the hospital workers. But even Father Antero acknowledged the robes did nothing to prevent the spread of the pesky fleas that seemed to be everywhere in the hospital. The fleas were, of course, the real cause of the plague—and Father Antero did contract the disease but recovered. He says,

> I have to change my clothes frequently if I do not want to be devoured by the fleas, armies of which nest in my gown, nor have I force enough to resist them, and I need great strength of mind to keep still at the altar. . . .
>
> Reader take pity on me, in the greatest of my sufferings. I can swear to you that all the bodily torments which are of necessity suffered in the [hospital] cannot compare even to the fleas, for they do not leave me alone even in the coldest depths of winter.

Quoted in Wendy Orent, *Plague: The Mysterious Past and Terrifying Future of the World's Most Dangerous Disease*. New York: Free Press, 2004, pp. 162–63.

of various aromas to ward off the plague. To fill their homes with these odors people burned exotic woods in their fireplaces. Some doctors believed the plague could be induced to leave through open windows, advising their patients which windows to open in their homes depending on the season and the positions of the sun and stars.

Some doctors preached sanitation. While little was done by the *Signori* to rid their cities of the filth that attracted the rats, some doctors recommended people pay closer attention to personal hygiene. However, clean water was not easy to come by in the cities of Renaissance Italy. Most people relied on rivers, public wells, or fountains to obtain their water. It was the task of the housewife to carry a jug to the local river, well, or fountain to obtain her home's daily supply of water. After filling the jug, the woman had to carry the water home on her head. A jug of water was heavy, and therefore, carrying it was a difficult task for a woman. Many women found it much easier to take their laundry or dishes to the public water supply and do their washing there. With everyone washing their dishes or clothes in the same wells or fountains, the water left behind could turn rancid.

The same was true for rivers, even though they enjoyed a steady current. Still, with horses, oxen, and other animals dropping their dung on the streets, whenever it rained that waste inevitably found its way into the river. Therefore, river water was often as foul as water in the wells. Still, doctors recommended washing hands—but this was also ineffective because it did nothing to prevent flea bites. Yet another measure advocated by doctors was to cover the mouth and nose in the presence of plague victims. Among the nose and mouth coverings advocated by doctors were bread or sponges soaked in vinegar or rose water. Again, these measures failed to prevent flea bites and were therefore ineffective.

Yet many doctors practiced these methods themselves and were able to remain in close contact with their patients without contracting the plague. Samuel K. Cohn Jr., a historian at the University of Glasgow in Scotland, suggests that doctors may have unknowingly built up immunities to the plague, and their meager efforts at sanitation were ineffective. "The proof of their methods, at least as far as they and their patients were concerned, was their own survival," says Cohn. "No doubt it had less to do with their recipes than their bodies' immune systems adapting to the new toxic germ."[36]

The *Becchini*

With doctors virtually powerless to stop the spread of the plague, in the cities struck by the disease—and virtually all Italian cities were afflicted—

When plagues ravaged cities, officials passed ordinances meant to keep healthy citizens away from the afflicted. Because of the warnings, families routinely pushed plague-ridden corpses out into the streets. There they would be picked up by becchini for disposal.

the stench of decaying bodies could be unbearable. Families dragged their deceased loved ones out of their homes, leaving them in the streets. They were collected by the grave diggers, the *becchini*. Despite the danger of contracting the plague there was rarely a shortage of men willing to serve as becchini, for the pay was very good. City and town officials, anxious to rid their streets of decaying bodies, were willing to pay whatever the becchini demanded.

Typically, a team of grave diggers pulled a cart through the streets, collecting the dead and piling the bodies atop one another. Priests led the procession through the streets, reciting prayers. Boccaccio describes a typical funeral procession:

> It was common practice of most of the neighbors, moved no less by fear of contamination by the putrefying bodies than by charity towards the deceased, to drag corpses out of the houses with their hands . . . and to lay them in front of the doors, where anyone who made the rounds might see them, especially in the morning, more of them than he could count; afterwards, they would have biers [wooden stands] brought up. . . . Nor was it once or twice only that one and the same bier carried two or three corpses at once, but quite a considerable number of such cases occurred, father and son, and so forth. And times without number it happened that, as two priests bearing the cross were on their way to perform that last office for someone, three or four biers were brought up by the porters in the rear, so that whereas the priests supposed that they had but one corpse to bury, they discovered that there were six or eight, or sometimes more.[37]

Outside the city or town limits, the becchini dug shallow pits where they dumped the bodies. Often, dogs and other animals could easily dig through the loose earth, pulling corpses out of the ground. Perhaps knowing that they would inevitably contract the plague, after completing their duties the becchini were known to spend their pay on drink and prostitutes. Many of them also turned to crime, robbing houses with the knowledge that homeowners would not put up a struggle against men who could already be infected with the Black Death.

Looking Back

In Venice, Commerce Before Caution

Venice was a city that relied on commerce with other Italian cities as well as foreign lands to feed its people and to supply residents with raw materials and other basic necessities. In 1575, as a new outbreak of plague threatened Venice, the city government cut off trade—worried that docking merchant vessels could be carrying the disease. The ban was soon lifted, though, because of the economic hardships faced by Venetians. Nevertheless, some sixty-four thousand Venetians—a third of the population of the city—died of the plague in the outbreak that lasted from 1575 to 1577. Says British historian Sheila Hale:

> The government was thus in a no-win situation. Banning industry and trade would depress the economy, reduce the wealth of merchants and manufacturers (many of them members of the governing class) and inflate the numbers of the starving poor by creating mass unemployment. Failure to [lift the trade embargo] could result in . . . thousands of deaths. . . . Representatives from [the city of] Verona, on which a blockade had been imposed after a severe outbreak of plague in September, were successful in persuading the [Venetian government] that such preventive measures were more harmful than the plague itself.

Sheila Hale, *Titian: His Life*. New York: HarperCollins, 2012, p. 710.

End of the Plague

The plague disappeared as mysteriously as it arrived. Although the disease made periodic returns to Europe until the early 1700s, the plague evidently died out on its own. Certainly, no medical cures were discovered during the Renaissance years.

Western civilization survived the plague. The cities and cultures that grew during the Renaissance years remained intact, even if many of the homes were left vacant after entire families succumbed to the illness. And although Titian and many of the other great achievers of the Renaissance were lost to the plague, many others did survive, helping to propel humankind into the modern world.

Chapter Five

Lives of the Artists

Perhaps the most significant achievement of the Italian Renaissance is the art produced during the era. Today the *Mona Lisa* and *The Last Supper* by Leonardo da Vinci, and the paintings that adorn the ceiling of the Sistine Chapel, and the sculpture of the ancient Hebrew king David by Michelangelo are considered among the greatest artistic accomplishments in history. Dozens of other Italian Renaissance artists—among them Titian; Sandro Botticelli; Raffaello Sanzio, better known as Raphael; and Donato di Niccolò di Betto Bardi, better known as Donatello—are regarded as masters as well. Says Will Durant,

> Artists took Nature into the studio, or betook themselves to Nature; nothing human or natural seemed in their view alien to art, no face so ugly but art could reveal its illuminating significance. They recorded the world; and . . . the painters left behind them the line and color, the life and passion, of the Renaissance.[38]

During the Renaissance era the works of art produced by these masters were greatly admired, but the profession of the artist was rarely a glamorous or lucrative field. Most artists of the Renaissance era were no more than hardworking members of the middle class. They were considered craftsmen on the same level as the goldsmiths, saddle makers, and shoemakers. They belonged to guilds that set prices for their work, much as the craft guilds did for their members. Most Renaissance artists earned their livings through commissions paid by wealthy customers seeking works of art to display in their *palazzi*. Other major customers were churches and the organizations of the era, such as guilds, which may have hired artists to create banners for parades. Major houses of commerce, such as banks, may have commissioned sculptures or paintings to decorate their places of business.

Some artists were supported by patrons—the wealthiest of the patricians and members of the nobility. Their financial backing helped keep the artists busy and producing some of the greatest paintings and sculptures of the Renaissance. Says Bruce Cole, the former chair of the National Endowment for the Humanities, which provides government assistance for the arts in America,

> The wealthy private patron commissioned artists for scores of items ranging from frescoes for the church to *cassoni* for the bedroom. The splendor and richness of his house and chapel enhanced his prestige and power. If he were a prince or duke, then his patronage and his image were of importance far beyond the city: what one commissioned was a fair indication of what one was.[39]

Veteran artists, known as masters or maestros, were responsible for the business side of their studios. The maestro had to buy paints and other supplies, pay the bills, negotiate with clients, plan the jobs, and find a way to make sure the studio remained profitable, often by obtaining commissions and sponsors. In other words, the art maestros of the Renaissance era were little different from the owners of small businesses found in contemporary society.

WORDS IN CONTEXT

maestro

An artist who owns a studio and employs apprentices, who provide menial chores for the studio while learning the craft of the artist.

Apprentice Artists

Long before the artist reached the point of seeking a commission or the sponsorship of a wealthy patron, however, he had to learn his trade. Typically, boys were apprenticed to maestros, with whom they spent years learning the techniques of painting and sculpture. Girls were not permitted to enter the artistic fields, just as they were not permitted to take up the other trades.

Most boys began their apprenticeships in their early teen years. Cennino Cennini, a fifteenth-century artist and author from Padua, wrote

The thirteenth-century artist Cimabue watches a young Giotto drawing on a rock. Giotto served an apprenticeship with Cimabue, who instructed Giotto in painting.

an instructional guide for artists titled *The Craftsman's Handbook.* In it he explains the lure of the artistic fields:

> It is not without the impulse of a lofty spirit that some are moved to enter this profession, attractive to them through natural enthusiasm. Their intellect will take delight in drawing, provided their nature attracts them to it of themselves, without any master's guidance, out of loftiness of spirit. And then, through this delight, they come to want to find a master; and they bind themselves to him with respect for authority, undergoing an apprenticeship in order to achieve perfection in all this. There are those who pursue it, because of poverty and domestic need, for profit and enthusiasm for the

profession too; but above all these are to be extolled the ones who enter the profession through a sense of enthusiasm and exaltation.[40]

Menial Tasks

Boys who were apprenticed to maestros had not necessarily shown a special talent for art. Since painting and sculpture were regarded as trades, to work in a maestro's studio boys needed no more talent in art than apprentices to saddle makers or shoemakers needed to show early talents in those trades. In most cases, maestros made apprentices out of their sons or parents found jobs for their boys in neighborhood studios. Says Cole, "Previously demonstrated talent, it appears, was not an overriding factor."[41]

Apprentice artists had plenty to do and learn. They had to learn how to mix paints to make the colors the maestro demanded, make paintbrushes and other tools, provide preliminary sketches, prepare the wood panels that were used for the actual works of art, and apply plaster to walls on which frescoes were painted. There were also dozens of menial tasks: sweeping the floors, running errands, erecting scaffolding at the job sites outside the studio, and unloading supplies—which could include heavy chunks of marble for sculpting.

> **WORDS IN CONTEXT**
> **scaffolding**
> Raised platforms, erected with wooden timbers, on which artists could stand to work on frescoes many feet above floor level.

As the young artist learned his craft, he was schooled in the techniques of painting and sculpture favored by the maestro. Eventually—sometimes after years of apprenticeship—the maestro might permit the apprentice to perform more serious work. Perhaps the artist-in-training might be permitted to work on a painting started by the maestro, or perhaps the maestro permitted the apprentice to take on an entire job.

Talents Flower Under the Maestros

Even though many of these boys had shown no talent for art prior to joining a studio, the system seemed to work, for it produced some of

Looking Back

Charming Caterina

When Leonardo da Vinci arrived in Milan to accept the post of court artist to Duke Ludovico Sforza, one member of the duke's court who found his charm infectious was Caterina Riario Sforza de' Medici. Caterina was the illegitimate daughter of Galeazzo Sforza, Ludovico's predecessor, and the wife of Giovanni di Bicci de' Medici, who represented the city of Florence as ambassador to Ludovico's court. Elizabeth Lev, an American-born art historian who makes her home in Rome, describes how Leonardo charmed and dazzled Caterina:

> By far the most fascinating member of Ludovico's . . . court was a Florentine artist named Leonardo da Vinci. He had come to Milan . . . bearing a gift from Lorenzo [de' Medici]: a silver lyre of in the shape of a horse's head. His talent at playing the instrument and composing songs delighted the music-loving court, and his remarkable abilities as a military engineer, architect, and artist had obtained him a job.
>
> [Leonardo] turned heads with his physical beauty. Boasting long, flowing hair, he was lithe and strong and his every move had the graceful ease of an athlete. . . . Caterina must have delighted in the charm of the artist, who also loved horses as much as she did. Leonardo frequented the duke's innermost circle and Caterina would have heard him entertaining the court with word games or outlining plans for his latest project.

Elizabeth Lev, *The Tigress of Forli: Renaissance Italy's Most Courageous and Notorious Countess, Caterina Riario Sforza de' Medici*. New York: Houghton Mifflin Harcourt, 2011, p. 107.

history's greatest artists. Florentine painter and author Giorgio Vasari, who in 1550 authored a history of Renaissance art titled *Lives of the Artists*, told many stories of how the talents of apprentices flowered under their maestros. One of Vasari's stories involves the emergence of fourteenth-century Florentine artist Giotto di Bondone under the guidance of his maestro, Bencivieni di Pepo, known as Cimabue: "It is said that when Giotto was still a young man with Cimabue, he once painted upon the nose of a figure that Cimabue had completed a fly which looked so natural that when his master returned to continue his work, he tried more than once to drive the fly away with his hand, convinced that it was real, before he realized his mistake."[42]

Eventually, the apprentices moved on to seek work on their own. Typically, before establishing their own studios young artists at the beginning of their careers traveled in search of commissions. "Their livelihood was based on obtaining commissions; consequently they were willing, and indeed eager, to work almost anywhere,"[43] says Cole.

From City to City

As they arrived in each new city to begin work on commissioned projects, the traveling artists faced many challenges. They had to find places to live. They may have had to hire assistants, particularly if they were commissioned to paint frescoes, which often required the erection of scaffolding. They had to find suppliers of paints—or, if they were sculptors, they needed to procure bronze and marble—and negotiate prices with these merchants.

At times the artists also had to contend with interference by forceful and controlling clients. Vasari relates the troubles endured by Pietro Perugino, a painter from Perugia, as he worked on a commission in Florence. Perugino was commissioned to create numerous frescoes of New Testament scenes on the walls of the San Giovannino Catholic church. According to Vasari, the prior of the church supplied

Perugino with the paints he required for the commission and, evidently, had purchased an overabundance of ultramarine—a shade of deep blue. The prior demanded that Perugino use as much ultramarine as possible, and to make sure Perugino followed his orders insisted on being present as the artist applied the color to the walls. The prior also insisted on doling out the ultramarine to Perugino.

The artist regarded the prior's presence as he worked an insult. And so he concocted a plan to deceive the prior by rinsing off his brush after every two brush strokes, which helped dilute the pigment before he applied it to the wall. The prior believed the plaster was absorbing the ultramarine and left to retrieve a new supply of the paint. When the prior returned, Perugino showed the prior all the ultramarine that had accumulated in the bottom of the wash basin. Perugino told the prior, "Father, this is yours: now learn to trust honest men who never deceive those who trust them but who know how very well, if they wish, to deceive suspicious men such as yourself."[44] The prior accepted Perugino's admonishment to leave the art to the artist, and Perugino went on to win numerous other commissions from churches throughout Italy, adorning their walls with frescoes.

Cosimo and Donatello

For the Renaissance artists, the patronage of a wealthy patrician or noble meant they could avoid many of the demands made by clients like those suffered by Perugino. Wealthy patrons were willing to provide generous commissions, for they knew their own social standings were heightened by the art adorning their *palazzi*, the churches where they worshipped, or their houses of commerce. Cosimo de' Medici supported many artists, particularly the sculptor Donatello, while the artist was still young and unknown. Cosimo provided patronage to Donatello until Cosimo's death in 1464. And nearing death, he instructed his son Piero to continue to support Donatello. Says Durant,

Patron and artist grew old together, and Cosimo took such care of the sculptor that Donatello rarely thought about money. He

Pope Julius II ascends scaffolding in the Sistine Chapel to talk with Michelangelo. The artist would become a prime mover in the Renaissance, influencing artists to adopt a style of figure painting and sculpture that embraced movement, expression, and perspective.

kept his funds . . . in a basket suspended from the ceiling of his studio, and bade his aides and friends to take it according to their needs, without consulting him. When Cosimo was dying he recommended Donatello to the care of his son Piero; Piero gave the old artist a house in the country, but Donatello soon returned to Florence, preferring his accustomed studio to the sunshine and insects of the countryside.[45]

Artist and Musician

Another young artist whose work was discovered by a wealthy patron was Leonardo da Vinci. Da Vinci's immense talent was recognized at an early age by another Medici, Cosimo's grandson Lorenzo. Starting in the 1460s Leonardo apprenticed in the Florentine studio of maestro Andrea del Verrocchio. Under del Verrocchio's guidance, da Vinci developed a keen eye for perspective: the accuracy in depth and distance found in fine art. Da Vinci's interest in perspective led to his study of geometry and other mathematical fields.

But it was his skill as an artist that brought him to the attention of Lorenzo, who by then was so powerful that he was regarded as the virtual ruler of Florence. Lorenzo the Magnificent, as he was known, accepted Leonardo into his circle of friends and enjoyed Leonardo's talents not only as an artist but as a musician. Leonardo was an exceptional lyre player and is also said to have had a melodious singing voice. Lorenzo rewarded Leonardo with many commissions, enabling him in 1477 to leave Verrocchio's studio and set up his own.

WORDS IN CONTEXT
Lyre
A small, stringed musical instrument similar to a harp.

In 1479 Lorenzo sent a number of artists to Rome to provide paintings and frescoes for the Vatican. Leonardo was not among them. By then he had fallen out of Lorenzo's favor because he had developed a reputation as an artist who often did not complete his paintings—angering Lorenzo and other wealthy patricians and nobles who had awarded him commissions.

In Their Own Words

Advice for the Young Artist

In his instructional guide for artists, *The Craftsman's Handbook*, the fifteenth-century artist and author Cennino Cennini provided some practical advice for apprentices, specifically how they should conduct themselves while in the service of their maestros. For example, he advised them on diet, physical labor, and relations with women. He says,

> Your life should always be arranged just as if you were studying theology, or philosophy, or other theories, that is to say, eating and drinking moderately, at least twice a day, electing digestible and wholesome dishes, and light wines; saving and sparing your hand, preserving it from such strains as heaving stones, crowbar, and many other things which are bad for your hand, from giving them a chance to weary it. There is another cause which, if you indulge it, can make your hand so unsteady that it will waver more, and flutter far more, than leaves do in the wind, and that is indulging too much in the company of a woman.

Daniel V. Thompson Jr., trans., *The Craftsman's Handbook by Cennino Cennini*. New York: Dover, 1960, p. 16.

Treacherous Waters of State

One hundred fifty miles south of Florence political events were unfolding that helped Leonardo find a new patron and, eventually, led to Leonardo painting one of the world's greatest works of art: *The Last Supper*.

These events were unfolding in the city of Milan. Unlike Florence and other Italian Renaissance cities, Milan was not governed by a *Signoria* but rather fell under the rule of the Sforza family.

The first Sforza duke to rule, Francesco, raised an army and conquered the city in 1450. He was succeeded in 1466 by his son Galeazzo, a cruel despot who was assassinated in 1476 by three rival aristocrats. The throne then fell to Galeazzo's seven-year-old son, Giangaleazzo. Too young to rule, the chores of administering the government fell to the boy's uncle, Ludovico, who served as regent until 1494. When Giangaleazzo died that same year, rumors swirled throughout the city that Ludovico had him poisoned just as the boy turned twenty-five and became old enough to claim the throne as duke. Following his nephew's death Ludovico accepted the title of duke.

Throughout the period of his regency, Ludovico had to navigate through the treacherous waters of state. His authority was opposed by the rulers of Naples and Venice. To protect Milan from invasion by his enemies, Ludovico appealed for protection to the French king Charles VIII. Charles readily agreed, since a treaty with Milan provided French armies with an uncontested means of entering northern Italy and laying siege to France's enemies.

Leonardo Arrives in Milan

Leonardo learned of the perilous political situation facing the duke of Milan. He wrote a letter to Ludovico offering his services—not only as an artist, but as a skilled designer who could fashion new weapons for the duke's army. Leonardo felt his study of geometry and other mathematical fields qualified him to design weapons of war. His study of geometry had given Leonardo a working knowledge of measurement, angles, and the area of surfaces—all important components in the design of objects and buildings. In a letter to Ludovico, he writes,

> Most illustrious Lord, having now sufficiently seen and considered
> the proofs of all those who count themselves masters and inventors
> of instruments of war, and finding that their invention and use of

the said instruments does not differ in any respect from those in common practice, I am emboldened without prejudice to anyone else to put myself in communication with your Excellency, in order to acquaint you with my secrets, thereafter offering myself at your pleasure.[46]

Leonardo insisted in the letter that he could design ships that could resist fires during battles at sea; ladders to be used for scaling castle walls; bridges that could sustain the weight of any army; shelters for wagons that could withstand attack from enemy archers; canons and other firearms, as well as catapults, traps, and similar weapons. At the end of the letter Leonardo casually added that he was also an artist and offered to sculpt a bronze horse for the duke. "[It] shall endue with immortal glory and eternal honor the auspicious memory of the Prince your father and of the illustrious house of Sforza."[47]

In 1482 Ludovico sent for Leonardo—not to design weapons but for employment as the court artist. Among his duties were designing costumes for contestants in jousts, painting the portraits of horses to decorate stable walls, designing dresses and jewelry, and painting whatever portraits and murals the duke desired.

The Last Supper

Soon after Leonardo arrived in Milan, Ludovico summoned him and asked him to paint a rendition of the Last Supper—the final meal that, according to the Gospel, Jesus shared with his Apostles in Jerusalem before his crucifixion. He asked Leonardo to paint a mural of the scene on a wall in the refectory—the dining hall—where the friars of the Church of Santa Maria delle Grazie took their meals. Santa Maria delle Grazie was Ludovico's favorite church.

Leonardo did not begin the task until 1495 and did not finish until 1498. The friars expected the job to be finished in swift order and often complained to Ludovico about Leonardo's sloth. On some days, they told the duke, the artist did little more than spend hours staring at the wall. Vasari describes the frustration of the friars with Leonardo:

Leonardo da Vinci was summoned to Milan by Duke Ludovico Sforza, who employed him as a court artist. Under Ludovico's patronage, Leonardo painted The Last Supper *as well as sculpted several statues, including horse sculptures like the one shown in this sketch.*

It is said that the prior of the church entreated Leonardo with tiresome persistence to complete the work, since it seemed strange to him to see how Leonardo sometimes passed half a day at a time lost in thought, and he would have preferred Leonardo, just like the labourers hoeing in the garden, never to have laid down his brush. And if this was not enough, he complained to the duke and made such a disturbance that the duke was forced to send for Leonardo and to question him skillfully about his work, showing with great civility that he was doing so because of the prior's insistence.[48]

When Ludovico summoned the court artist for an explanation, Leonardo told the duke, "Men of genius do most when they work least."[49] Says Vasari, "This moved the duke to laughter, and the duke declared that Leonardo was quite right."[50] Leonardo also acknowledged during his meeting with Ludovico that he spent most of his time on the streets of Milan, examining the faces of the *milanesi*. He knew the gravity of the task he faced: to place human features on the images of Jesus and the Apostles. And so Leonardo roamed the streets, studying the features of ordinary men, making notes and sketches that he applied to the painting.

Eventually *The Last Supper* was completed, but the years left for Ludovico to enjoy Leonardo's masterpiece were brief. In 1499 Ludovico's French ally, Charles VIII, was succeeded by a new French monarch, Louis XII. Louis chose to ally himself with Ludovico's many enemies. The French moved against the duke, ousting him from the throne. He spent the remainder of his life a captive of the French and died in 1508.

Demands and Setbacks

After completing *The Last Supper* Leonardo went on to other triumphs—completing the *Mona Lisa* in 1517 and further pursuing his interest in geometry. He even designed an early version of a manned aircraft. He also found an opportunity to design weapons, serving as a military engineer for Cesare Borgia in 1502. But the financial success achieved by Leonardo and a few of his contemporaries, including Donatello, was the exception rather the rule.

For the most part, the artists of the Renaissance were little different than the merchants and artisans of the era. Typically they were born into families of modest circumstances, and they had to work hard to lift themselves out of their apprenticeships and establish their own studios, while enduring the demands and setbacks of commercial life during the Italian Renaissance.

Source Notes

Introduction: The Rebirth

1. Dorothy Sayers, trans., *The Divine Comedy 1: Hell*. Middlesex, UK: Penguin, 1973, p. 10.
2. Andrew Graham-Dixon, *Renaissance*. Berkeley: University of California Press, 1999, p. 12.
3. Quoted in Lauro Martines and Murtha Baca, *An Italian Renaissance Sextet: Six Tales in Historical Context*. Toronto, ON: University of Toronto Press, 2004, p. 163.

Chapter One: Patricians and Nobles of the Italian Renaissance

4. Will Durant, *The Renaissance: The Story of Civilization, Part V*. New York: Simon & Schuster, 1953, p. 75.
5. Quoted in Durant, *The Renaissance: The Story of Civilization*, p. 75.
6. William Manchester, *A World Lit by Fire: The Medieval Mind and the Renaissance*. Boston: Little, Brown, 1992, p. 74.
7. Quoted in Melissa Walton, "The Scandalous Reputation of Pope Alexander VI," *Clio*, 2007. https://cliojournal.wikispaces.com.
8. Quoted in Sarah Bradford, *Cesare Borgia: His Life and Times*. London: Penguin, 2011. Kindle edition.
9. Quoted in Durant, *The Renaissance: The Story of Civilization*, p. 422.
10. Durant, *The Renaissance: The Story of Civilization*, p. 439.
11. Quoted in Karl Federn, *Dante & His Time*. New York: Haskell House, 1970, p. 116.

Chapter Two: The Middle Class

12. William Shakespeare, *The Merchant of Venice*, Complete Works of William Shakespeare, Massachusetts Institute of Technology, 1993. http://shakespeare.mit.edu.
13. Sophus A. Reinert, ed., *A Short Treatise on the Wealth and Poverty of Nations by Antonio Serra*. London: Anthem, 2011, p. 35.
14. Durant, *The Renaissance: The Story of Civilization*, p. 282.

15. Quoted in John P. McKay, Bennett D. Hill, John Buckler, Clare Haru Crowston, Merry E. Wiesner-Hanks, and Joe Perry, *History of Western Society Since 1300*. Boston: Bedford/St. Martin's, 2011, p. 375.

16. Quoted in Evelyn Welch, *Shopping in the Renaissance: Consumer Cultures in Italy, 1400–1600*. New Haven, CT: Yale University Press, 2005, p. 81.

17. Quoted in Robyn Conway, "The Place of Women in Renaissance Italy and Women's Opportunities for Making a Life of Their Own," Academia.edu, 2015. www.academia.edu.

18. Quoted in William Eamon, *The Professor of Secrets: Mystery, Medicine, and Alchemy in Renaissance Italy*. Washington: National Geographic, 2010, p. 56.

19. Quoted in Piero Gambaccini, *Mountebanks and Medicasters: A History of Italian Charlatans from the Middle Ages to the Present*. Jefferson, NC: McFarland, 2004, pp. 105–106.

Chapter Three: The Lower Class

20. Quoted in Philip Gavitt, *Charity and Children in Renaissance Florence: The Ospedale degli Innocenti, 1410–1536*. Ann Arbor: University of Michigan Press, 1990, pp. 3–4.

21. Quoted in Gavitt, *Charity and Children in Renaissance Florence*, p. 9.

22. John K. Brackett, *Criminal Justice and Crime in Late Renaissance Florence, 1537–1609*. Cambridge: Cambridge University Press, 2002, p. 2.

23. Elizabeth Starr Cohen and Thomas Vance Cohen, *Daily Life in Renaissance Italy*. Westport, CT: Greenwood, 2001, p. 122.

24. Charles G. Nauert, *The A to Z of the Renaissance*. Langham, MD: Scarecrow, 2004, p. 366.

25. Quoted in Samuel Kline Cohn, *The Labouring Classes in Renaissance Florence*. New York: Academic Press, 1980, p. xiii.

26. Niccolò Machiavelli, *The History of Florence and the Prince*. London: Bohn, 1847, pp. 132–33.

27. Duccio Balestracci, *Renaissance in the Fields: Family Memoirs of a Fifteenth-Century Tuscan Peasant*. University Park: Pennsylvania State University Press, 1999, p. 63.

28. Quoted in John Rigby Hale, *Renaissance Europe: Individual and Society, 1480–1520*. Berkeley: University of California Press, 1977, p. 198.

Chapter Four: The Black Death

29. Quoted in P.M. Rogers, "Plague Readings," University of Arizona, 2002. www.u.arizona.edu.

30. Quoted in Robert Sullivan, *Rats: Observations on the History & Habitat of the City's Most Unwanted Inhabitants.* New York: Bloomsbury, 2004, p. 139.

31. Quoted in Garry Wills, *Venice, Lion City: The Religion of an Empire.* New York: Simon & Schuster, 2001, p. 263.

32. Carlo M. Cipolla, *Fighting the Plague in Seventeenth-Century Italy.* Madison: University of Wisconsin Press, 1981, p. 14.

33. Giovanni Boccaccio, *The Project Gutenberg EBook of the Decameron of Giovanni Boccaccio,* Project Gutenberg, 2007. www.gutenberg.org.

34. Wills, *Venice, Lion City,* 2001, p. 263.

35. Quoted in Wendy Orent, *Plague: The Mysterious Past and Terrifying Future of the World's Most Dangerous Disease.* New York: Free Press, 2004, p. 163.

36. Samuel K. Cohn Jr., *Cultures of Plague: Medical Thinking at the End of the Renaissance.* Oxford: Oxford University Press, 2010. Kindle edition.

37. Quoted in Robert S. Gottfried, *Black Death: Natural and Human Disaster in Medieval Europe.* New York: Free Press, 1985, p. 47.

Chapter Five: Lives of the Artists

38. Durant, *The Renaissance: The Story of Civilization,* p. 134.

39. Bruce Cole, *The Renaissance Artist at Work: From Pisano to Titian.* Boulder, CO: Westview, 1983, p. 49.

40. Daniel V. Thompson Jr., trans., *The Craftsman's Handbook by Cennino Cennini.* New York: Dover, 1960, pp. 2–3.

41. Cole, *The Renaissance Artist at Work,* p. 33.

42. Quoted in Julia Conaway, *Giorgio Vasari: The Lives of the Artists.* Oxford, UK: Oxford University Press, 1991. Kindle version.

43. Cole, *The Renaissance Artist at Work,* p. 33.

44. Quoted in Conaway, *Giorgio Vasari.*

45. Durant, *The Renaissance: The Story of Civilization,* p. 95.

46. Quoted in Durant, *The Renaissance: The Story of Civilization,* p. 202.

47. Quoted in Durant, *The Renaissance: The Story of Civilization,* p. 203.

48. Conaway, *Giorgio Vasari.*

49. Quoted in Durant, *The Renaissance: The Story of Civilization,* p. 205.

50. Quoted in Conaway, *Giorgio Vasari.*

For Further Research

Books

Ole J. Benedictow, *The Black Death, 1346–1353: The Complete History*. Suffolk, UK: Boydell, 2012.

Ross King and Anja Grebe, *Florence: The Paintings and Frescoes*. New York: Black Dog & Leventhal, 2015.

G.J. Meyer, *The Borgias: The Hidden History*. New York: Bantam, 2014.

Loren Partridge, *Art of Renaissance Venice, 1400–1600*. Oakland: University of California Press, 2015.

H. Anna Suh, ed., *Leonardo's Notebooks: Writing and Art of the Great Master*. New York: Black Dog & Leventhal, 2013.

Websites

Dante Alighieri (www.greatdante.net). The website devoted to the life of Renaissance poet Dante Alighieri provides students with a biography of Dante as well as an overview of his works. Students can download many of Dante's poems, including *The Divine Comedy*. Biographies of other Renaissance figures, such as Giovanni Boccaccio, are available on the site as well.

Medici: Godfathers of the Renaissance (www.pbs.org/empires/medici). The companion website to the 2005 PBS documentary series chronicles the most powerful family of the Italian Renaissance. Students can find information on the art, architecture, and science of the Renaissance as well as biographies of Medici family members.

Mystery of the Black Death (www.pbs.org/wnet/secrets/mystery-black-death-background/1488). The companion website to the 2015 PBS documentary *Mystery of the Black Death* provides an overview of the bubonic plague that wiped out millions of Europeans. The site includes an interview with genetic scientist Stephen J. O'Brien of the National Institutes of Health, who provides a biological explanation for the disease.

Palazzo Davanzati (www.museumsinflorence.com/musei/palazzo_davanzati.html). The former palace of the Davanzati family in Florence is now maintained as a museum. Visitors to the museum's website can find a description of the mansion as well as floor plans, drawings, and photographs of what was once one of Renaissance Italy's most luxurious homes.

Sistine Chapel (http://mv.vatican.va/3_EN/pages/CSN/CSN_Main.html). Sponsored by the Vatican Museums in Rome, the website relates how Michelangelo created the frescoes that tell the story of Genesis on the ceiling of the Sistine Chapel in Rome. Visitors to the website can observe images of the frescoes.

Internet Sources and Periodicals

Black Death. www.bbc.co.uk/history/british/middle_ages/black_01.shtml.

Robyn Conway, "The Place of Women in Renaissance Italy and Women's Opportunities for Making a Life of their Own," Academia.edu, 2015. www.academia.edu/5490471/The_Place_of_Women_in_Renaissance_Italy_and_Womens_Opportunities_for_Making_a_Life_of_their_Own.

The Death of Pope Alexander VI, 1503, Eyewitness to History. www.eyewitnesstohistory.com/alexanderVI.htm.

Venetian Painting in the Early Renaissance. www.nga.gov/content/ngaweb/features/slideshows/venetian-painting-in-the-early-renaissance.html.

William Shakespeare's *Merchant of Venice*. http://shakespeare.mit.edu/merchant/full.html.

Index

Note: Boldface page numbers indicate illustrations.

Picture Credits

Cover: © Heritage Images/Corbis

Accurate Art, Inc.: 12

Akg-images/Tristan Lafranchis/Newscom: 68

© Alinari Archives/Corbis: 39

© Stefano Bianchetti/Corbis: 79

© Corbis: 84

Depositphotos: 8, 9, 31

© Christian Gautier/Biosphoto/Corbis: 60

© Alfredo Dagli Orti/The Art Archive/Corbis: 56

© Tondini Domenico/Hemis/Corbis: 51

© Tino Soriano/National Geographic Creative/Corbis: 25

© Summerfield Press/Corbis: 17

Carnival in Venice, by Hieronymus Francken I, painting/De Agostini Picture Library/A. Dagli Orti/Bridgeman Images: 27

Leg amputation, from the 'Field-book of wound surgery', 1530 (hand-coloured woodcut), Gersdorff, Hans von (fl. 16th century)/Private Collection/Joerg Hejkal /Bridgeman Images: 42

Peasants Brawling, 1619 (oil on panel), Brueghel, Pieter the Younger (c.1564–1638)/Private Collection/Photo © Christie's Images/ Bridgeman Images: 46

Doctor treating plague victims, Saint Sebastian's life (15th century), frescoes, Chapel of St Sebastian, Villard-de-Lans, Rhone-Alpes, France. Detail./De Agostini Picture Library/Bridgeman Images: 64

Cimabue observing the young Giotto drawing a goat on a rock, Sabatelli, Gaetano (fl. 1842–93)/Galleria d'Arte Moderna, Florence, Italy/Bridgeman Images: 74

About the Author

Hal Marcovitz is a former newspaper reporter and columnist who makes his home in Chalfont, Pennsylvania. He is the author of nearly two hundred books for young readers. His other titles in the Living History series are *Life in the Time of Shakespeare* and *Life in Nazi Germany*.